POWER

for
Cubase 5

HAL LEONARD BOOKS
An Imprint of Hal Leonard Corporation | New York

Brian McConnon

Published in 2010 by Hal Leonard Books
An Imprint of Hal Leonard Corporation
7777 West Bluemound Road
Milwaukee, WI 53213

Trade Book Division Editorial Offices
19 West 21st Street, New York, NY 10010

www.halleonard.com

Book design by Kristina Rolander
Front cover design by Richard Slater

Library of Congress Cataloging-in-Publication Data

McConnon, Brian.
 Power tools for Cubase 5 / Brian McConnon.
    p. cm.
 Includes index.
 ISBN 978-1-4234-7453-1
 1. Cubase 2. Digital audio editors. I. Title.
 ML74.4.C8M33 2010
 781.3'4536--dc22
                                              2009051745

Printed in the United States of America

Acknowledgments

I would like to thank the many people who contributed to and supported me in the writing of this book. Thanks to Rusty Cutchin and John Cerullo of Hal Leonard Publishing for giving me the opportunity to write the book. Thanks to my wife Martina for encouraging me to take on such a monstrous task and, along with my children Colin and Ella, giving me the time and space to complete it. For their hospitality during my trip to Hamburg and their contributions, thanks to those at Steinberg Media Technologies AG: Andreas Mazurkiewics, Andreas Stelling, Angus Baigent, Arnd Kaiser, Dave Nicholson, Frank Simmerlein, Klaus Mueller, Paul Grathwohl, and Stefan Schreiber. Thanks to the Cubase "power users" who took time out of their busy professional lives to be interviewed for the book: Brent Bodrug, Chris "The Greek" Panaghi, Fritz Hilpert and Kraftwerk, Jochem van der Saag, Joris de Man, Paul Mirkovich, Rick DePofi, Steve Lamm, and Vince Melamed. Thanks to Brian McGovern of Steinberg North America for his support with hardware and software. Thanks to Greg Ondo of Steinberg North America for his technical expertise and consultation throughout the book and his contributions to Chapter 13. Finally, a special thanks to Charlie Steinberg and Manfred Rürup for their interview and for creating a company and a platform that has helped millions of people throughout the world make and record their music.

Contents

Introduction

Computer-based digital audio workstations (DAWs) have developed over the past 25 years in parallel with the evolution of the personal computer. With each technological leap forward — faster computer processors and system buses, increased random-access memory (RAM), greater hard drive storage capacity, and wider bandwidth — DAW developers eagerly squeezed out every drop of newfound power, in the end delivering capabilities that were once solely the domain of multimillion-dollar commercial studios to any musician with a computer and a few hundred bucks. Steinberg Media Technologies was an early pioneer of MIDI sequencing and digital audio recording on the personal computer, and continues to be a leading innovator today. Steinberg's story is a living history of computer DAW development, culminating with the release of Cubase 5, the fifth and latest generation of the company's legendary line of music creation and production software.

In the first half of the 1980s, with the personal computer still in its infancy, the limitations of computer processing power meant that most digital audio recording was done on tape machines, so developers quickly made the most of the burgeoning and less CPU-intensive MIDI protocol to bring powerful MIDI sequencing to the computer. Founded in 1984 with a crude but effective MIDI interface and rudimentary software conceived by working musicians, Steinberg was among the early leaders of computer MIDI sequencing. Before long, computer step-sequencers could not only do more than their dedicated hardware counterparts, but do it within a user interface that made sequencing faster, easier, and naturally linear.

Toward the end of the '80s and throughout the '90s, computer processing began to accelerate exponentially, providing enough power for digital audio to be recorded alongside MIDI in multitrack recording projects. By the mid-'90s, Steinberg had succeeded in bringing a complete recording studio to the desktop in Cubase VST, enabling a new generation of musicians to make creative, professional-quality recordings.

In the 2000s, developers raced to take advantage of the great leaps in computer power, adding more tracks, more features, more effects, and better hardware interfaces. The "feature wars" were in full swing, and by early 2000, computer processing had advanced to the point that DAWs could do virtually anything a home recordist—or, for that matter, a project studio or commercial facility—could want. Features included unlimited tracks, unlimited undos, real-time digital signal processing, print-quality scoring, more effects than a studio full of outboard gear, and more. Also, an explosion in the speed and popularity of laptop computers made everything increasingly portable.

DAW development then shifted from a focus on features to a focus on workflow—making recording easier, faster, and more customized to users' needs. The proliferation of ready-made content and loop-based recording created a whole new way of working. Collaboration and the Internet made communication and file portability essential. And a preference for hardware-controlled software environments made compatibility and integration paramount. Steinberg leapt ahead in all these areas with a new generation of Cubase called SX. And over the past few years, its partnership with the Yamaha Corporation has yielded a number of integrated hardware and software solutions, while still keeping Cubase an open standard.

Today, musicians have just about any tool they can imagine at their fingertips. So where does the future of DAW development lie? In adaptability and scalability. It seems there is a new race on these days, and that is to provide the perfect audio solution for the wide variety of music now being created. This means that a DAW must be as at home in a film composer's studio as it is on a DJ's laptop, as capable in a remote recording truck as it is on stage. It means that more than ever, a DAW must be flexible in terms of file format exchange, and also integrate well with the hardware world. In short, a competitive DAW must be all things to all people in a world where audio has converged with many other types of media production to allow content to be created for new platforms and new consumers.

POWER TOOLS
FROM POWER USERS

Steinberg's Cubase 5 is the culmination of a quarter century of innovation in MIDI sequencing, audio recording, and technology development that has helped to transform the personal computer into a high-powered, versatile, and portable recording studio.

In this new incarnation of the Power Tools series, we will not only cover the many powerful new features of Cubase 5, providing descriptions and practical examples, but also highlight professional Cubase users to help demonstrate the various applications of the software. These "power users" depend on the software in their day-to-day work as composers, songwriters, remixers, audio engineers, and record producers.

Power Tools for Cubase 5 also includes exclusive interviews with Steinberg personnel, from the developers to the management team. They share their thoughts, experiences, and reasoning behind the new features in Cubase 5 and discuss how and why they were developed. A bonus chapter includes fifty tips, tricks, and suggestions to help you get the most from Cubase 5.

Lastly, a special section in commemoration of Steinberg's 25th anniversary provides a history of the company and its many innovative contributions to computer recording, and details the development of the Cubase line. It also includes rare interviews with key players in Steinberg's history, including founders Karl (Charlie) Steinberg and Manfred Rürup.

Cubase Basics

While Power Tools for Cubase 5 is intended for those of you with a working knowledge of the program, in this chapter I will cover some of the basic concepts, geography, and terminology of Cubase that will be used throughout the book. This section is not meant to be a complete tutorial, simply an overview of some of the more common Cubase features and procedures. If you're well versed in Cubase, you may want to jump to the chapters on the new features in Cubase 5; otherwise, read on for a refresher. If you are new to Cubase and would like a complete tutorial, there are many great resources available in print, including the Cubase 5 manual, and on the Internet.

The goal of Cubase, first released in 1989 for the Atari ST computer, is to transform the personal computer into a complete music creation and production studio, allowing the musician to take a piece of music from an idea to a final mix, all in one software application.

GET CONNECTED

The first thing you need to do to record audio on your computer is get the audio from your instrument or microphone into the computer, and be able to listen to what you've recorded by sending the audio back out. Cubase does this via input and output buses. Input buses route audio signals from your audio interface into

Cubase. Output buses route audio from the application back out to your audio interface. This can be done using audio interface hardware as simple as the microphone input and headphone output on your computer, or as complicated as a multichannel digital mixing console. Setting up the input and output buses in Cubase is done via the VST Connections window (see Fig. 1.1), which is accessed through the Devices menu. Once you have the driver for your audio interface installed, it will show up here. If you are using the built-in mic input and headphone output, you can select the Built-in Audio driver option.

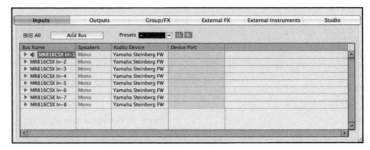

Fig. 1.1: The VST Connections window

CREATE A NEW PROJECT

Once your inputs and outputs are connected, you'll be able to start a new Project. The main screen in Cubase is called the Project window (see Fig. 1.2). The Project window is an overview

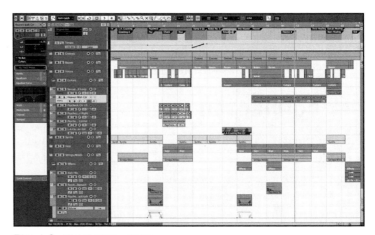

Fig. 1.2: The Project window

screen from which you can see a linear representation of your project over time as indicated by a timeline called the Ruler. Tracks are stacked vertically in the Project window and can be of several types, including audio, MIDI, folder, instrument, marker, tempo, and video. You can read about the different track types and their uses on page 26 of the *Cubase 5 Operation Manual*.

POWER TIP
Create a New Project and Add a Track

When opening Cubase 5, you will be asked to either open an existing Project or Template, or create an empty Project. The easiest way to get going is to open a Template. For this example, let's open an empty Project and add a track.

1. Launch Cubase 5, select New Project, then select Empty.
2. Choose the Project folder (where the project and data you record is to be stored).
3. Once the Project is open, go to the Project menu and select Add Track.
4. Select Audio and click OK.

You now have an audio track in your Project that is record-enabled and ready to go. You can repeat this process with any other type of track in Cubase, such as MIDI and VST instrument tracks.

GETTING AROUND A PROJECT

You may notice that different audio programs handle audio differently, if only in name. In Cubase, an audio file is called an Audio Clip, and clips are stored in the Audio Pool in their original recorded or imported form. Audio that is placed in and moved around the tracks in the timeline are called Audio Events. These audio events can be edited, copied, processed, and changed in various ways, but the original audio clip remains intact. This is how Cubase allows you to undo anything an unlimited number of times, without affecting the original audio file. Other events, such as MIDI events, video events, and automation events, work the same way, leaving the original file untouched. Regions comprise a selected area within an audio clip.

Fig. 1.3: The Track Inspector

On the left-hand side of the Project window is the Inspector (see Fig. 1.3). As its name suggests, the Inspector is where you'll find information about a selected track within the project. The Inspector only shows settings and parameters for one track at a time, so you must select the track in the timeline to display its information. The Inspector is an incredible time-saver, as you can quickly see track settings such as input and output routing, EQ, inserts, and sends, and adjust these settings without opening their dedicated windows. Other parameters that can be controlled from the Inspector include volume, pan, instrument, mute, solo, and more. Of course, you can always open up each parameter's dedicated window to see more comprehensive data or make fine adjustments. The Inspector will display different parameters depending on the type of track selected. Page 30 of the *Cubase Operation Manual* lists what parameters are included in the Inspector for each track type.

Perhaps the biggest time-saver in the Project window, and in the program in general, are contextual menus (see Fig. 1.4). These are found by simply right-clicking (Control-clicking on a Mac) when the mouse pointer is positioned in the area you are working in. Doing this will bring up menus that are pertinent to that part of Cubase, so you don't have to leave the area and go into a pull-down menu. For example, right-clicking when the mouse is positioned over a track in the timeline brings up the Tools menu, which contains the Select, Split, Glue, and Draw tools, among others. If you right-click when the mouse is positioned over the Inspector, you'll see a list of parameters that can be shown in this area. Experiment with this a bit by moving the mouse around the program and right-clicking. You'll not only find relevant tools, but also other screens lying deep under the hood of Cubase that house its powerful features.

AUDIO EFFECTS

Cubase comes with a number of high-quality audio effects (or FX) that can be applied to tracks in a number of ways. You can apply effects to a track via the Inspector, the Mixer, or a context-sensitive menu. From there, each can be opened and edited individually (see Fig. 1.5). There are two types of effects: inserts

Fig. 1.4: Contextual menu

and sends. Compressors and limiters are common insert effects that are literally inserted into the audio path of a track. Reverb, delay, and chorus are examples of common send effects, in which audio from a track is sent, or bused, out to the effects processor and returned via its own track in the Mixer. Send effects can process multiple tracks simultaneously while giving you control over how much of each track is processed.

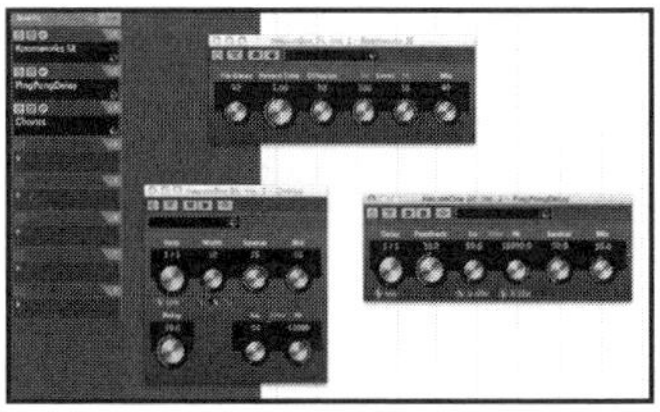

Fig. I.5: VST FX in the Inspector, open for editing

POWER TIP
Add an FX Track to Apply Reverb to an Audio Track

Earlier we set up a track for recording. After you have recorded on this track, this is how you can add an effects track and apply a simple reverb to it.

1. Go to the Project menu, select Add Track, and select FX Channel.

2. In the Add FX Channel track dialog, pull down the effect menu and select Reverb, then Roomworks SE.

3. Click OK to create the effects track.

4. Select your audio track and click on the Sends tab to open it.

5. Click on the first empty slot and select Roomworks SE.

6. Click on the On/Off icon in the upper left of the Send slot.

7. Use the slider at the bottom of the Send slot to adjust the volume of the reverb.

Now not only do you have reverb on your audio track, but you also have an independent effects track set up, so you can apply the same Roomworks SE reverb to other tracks.

VIRTUAL INSTRUMENTS

Virtual instruments, or VSTi's, are virtual models of real instruments such as synthesizers, drums, guitars, or any other type of instrument. Cubase comes with a number of VSTi's built into the program, and there are hundreds, if not thousands, of other VST instruments made by third-party companies. VSTi's are housed in a virtual rack within Cubase (see Fig. 1.6) and can be assigned via the Inspector or through the creation of an

Fig. 1.6: VSTi rack

instrument track. Once created, a VSTi can be played via MIDI input from an external keyboard, or with the built-in virtual keyboard.

POWER TIP
Add a VST Instrument and Play It from Within Cubase

1. Go to the Project menu, select Add Track, and select Instrument.

2. In the Add Instrument track dialog, pull down the instrument menu and select Synth, then Embracer.

3. Click OK to create an instrument track.

4. Right-click on the Transport Bar and select Virtual Keyboard.

5. With the Embracer instrument track selected, click the keys of the virtual keyboard to play the instrument.

This is a really fast way to get a VST instrument up and running. You can also connect a MIDI keyboard to Cubase to play the instruments in a more natural way.

EDITING

Cubase has several editors, which allow you to dig down into an event for further manipulation. Two common editors are the Sample Editor and the MIDI Editor. The Sample Editor (see Fig. 1.7) allows you to make more precise edits than is possible in the Project window. As in the Project window, you can cut, copy, and paste audio here, but you can also perform a number of deeper functions, such as real-time audio time stretching with the AudioWarp feature or pitch shifting with the new VariAudio feature (see chapter 3). You can zoom in to the single-sample level of a waveform, scrub back and forth to pinpoint a section of audio, and even draw in data to change the waveform.

The MIDI Editor is made up of several types of editors in which you can manipulate MIDI data. The main MIDI editor is called the Key Editor (see Fig. 1.8), which stacks MIDI data vertically on a timeline to correspond with the notes of a piano keyboard.

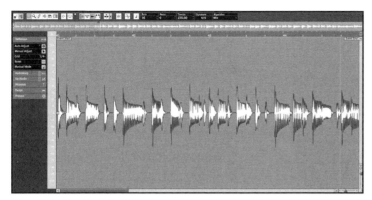

Fig. 1.7: The Sample Editor

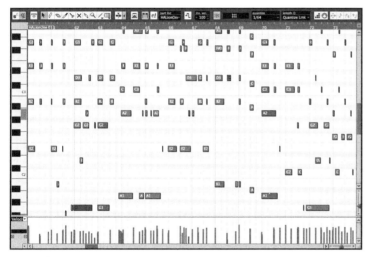

Fig. 1.8: The Key Editor

Notes can be played or drawn in the timeline and then freely moved in time or pitch, shortened or lengthened, made louder or softer, and so on. Other MIDI editors include the Drum Editor and the List Editor. As its name suggests, the Drum Editor (see Fig. 1.9) stacks notes in the timeline to correspond with drum parts instead of the notes on a piano keyboard. As would follow, the List Editor (see Fig. 1.10) shows MIDI events and parameters in numeric values, and these can be manipulated by changing the values to correspond to what you want to hear upon playback.

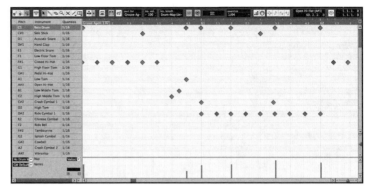

Fig. 1.9: The Drum Editor

Fig. 1.10: The List Editor

POWER TIP
Move MIDI Notes and Adjust Velocities in the Key Editor

The most common types of MIDI editing you will most likely do are moving the notes in time or in pitch and adjusting the velocity, or volume, of a note. You will want to move notes if you have played a wrong pitch or played a note too early or late. You'll want to adjust the velocity if you need single notes to be louder or softer.

1. Open a project that contains MIDI or instrument tracks (such as the demo songs that came with Cubase 5).

2. In the timeline, double-click on a MIDI track to open the Key Editor.

3. Click on the desired note and move it up or down to change the pitch, or left and right to change the timing.

4. In the controller lane (located below the notes), select Velocity from the pull-down menu on the left.

5. Click on the bar that lines up under the note you want to edit and move the bar up or down to change its velocity (volume).

MEDIABAY

One of the major workflow enhancements to Cubase that was added in Cubase 4 and enhanced shortly thereafter with VST Sound in Cubase 4.5 is the MediaBay. Much of music creation and production today involves assembling many different types of files together in a project. It's common to use audio file formats such as WAV, MP3, AIFF, and Windows Media in a single project as well as MIDI and REX files, and various types of video file formats. As you can imagine or may have experienced, finding the exact file you want to use when the creative moment strikes and then keeping track of these files once you find them can be a daunting task. VST Sound brings several features together to help you find, store, and retrieve media files on your computer quickly and easily.

It starts with the MediaBay (see Fig. 1.11), the media management system that gathers all the media files on your system including compatible outboard instruments as well as media files on attached storage devices. From here, you can browse all your different media files, tag and categorize them, and organize them in a familiar folder structure. You can then search for files by

Fig. 1.11: MediaBay

attribute in order to find the file types that fit what you need at a particular moment. For a more detailed discussion of MediaBay, see chapter 5.

POWER TIP
Search for a World Beat Drum Loop in MediaBay

For example, let's say you need a drum loop for a song that has a world beat feel to it. Because you have an idea of what you're looking for, MediaBay will help you find it by narrowing your search.

1. Go to the Media menu and select MediaBay (or press F5).

2. Under Category, select Drum&Perc.

3. Under Subcategory, select Beats.

4. Under Style, select World/Ethnic.

5. Audition the results by clicking the name once.

6. To add the loop to your project, double-click the name.

While this process may not always give you what you want or need, it's a very fast way of getting you in the ballpark and trying sounds and loops that might work. It's much faster than searching for files on your hard drive and then importing them to audition them.

The other components of VST Sound are VST loops, VST instruments, track presets, and VST3 presets. Cubase lets you tag and categorize any audio loops you want included in MediaBay. The VST instruments that come with Cubase, along with any third-party VST3-compatible virtual instruments, can also be searched within MediaBay, as can track presets (templates for audio tracks that include effects and mixer settings) and VST3 presets (a file containing all the parameter settings for a VST instrument or effect), giving you a very powerful way of organizing any and all media files within your Cubase system. Not only is this a great way to organize content, but it greatly enhances the creative process by allowing you to quickly find and audition any file on your computer.

THE POOL

The Pool stores the audio files that you record into Cubase's Project window (see Fig. 1.12). Earlier, we referred to these as audio clips. Think of the Pool as a "safe zone" where your original recorded audio clips remain untouched throughout the life of your project. This means that any edits you make to them in the Project window or Sample Editor will not affect them, making these edits nondestructive. The Pool is also where you can import audio, convert file formats, audition alternate takes of recorded audio, or prepare files for backup.

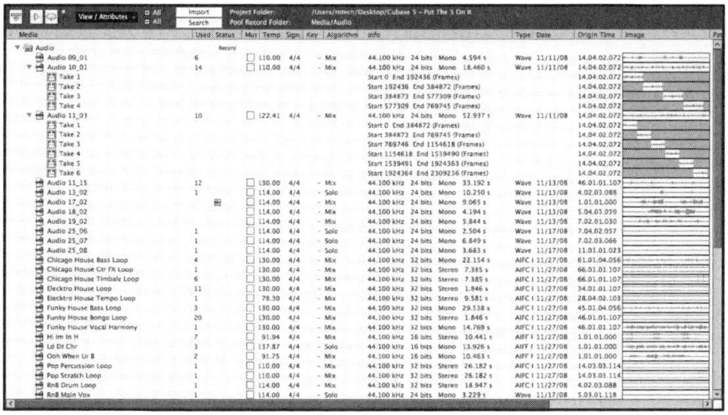

Fig. 1.12: The Pool

AUTOMATION

Automation is a topic that many view as too advanced, although it doesn't have to be. Simply put, automation records the various mixer adjustments you make for future playback. For example, if you want to make a fader adjustment to a track at a particular time in a song, simply enable the Write Automation button for that track and then record the fader move in real time as the song plays back. Then enable the Read Automation button for that track upon playback and Cubase will make the move for you every time. Another way to accomplish this is to open the Automation Lane from the Inspector and then draw in the change you want to make. This simple process can be done with many mixer parameters, including volume, pan, mute, tempo, and more. There are also more complicated things you can do with automation, but this is the basic concept, and some common automation tasks can save you time and editing. Cubase 5 adds many enhancements to automation, which are covered in chapter 4.

THE MIXER

The Mixer window will be familiar to most musicians because it looks very much like the analog mixers we've all used (see Fig. 1.13). Cubase has always done a great job of mimicking the analog world so that musicians are comfortable working in the virtual recording world. The Cubase mixer is scalable and can be configured in several different views to show and control a little or a lot at any given time. This is where you control each track's level, pan, inserts, FX, buses, and more. The mixer also allows you to control many types of tracks, such as audio, MIDI, effects, groups, and instruments. Most likely you'll spend most of your time in the Mixer once all of the recording and editing on your project has been done. You can access the Mixer window through the Devices menu or by pressing F3 on your keyboard.

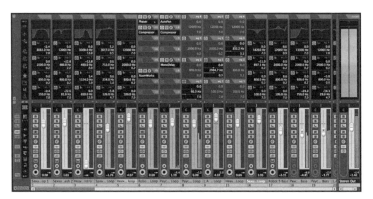

Fig. 1.13: The Mixer in extended view

CUBASE TERMINOLOGY

Steinberg is credited with creating many technologies that have become well-known standards in the computer recording industry. Terms like ASIO, VST, and VSTi have become so ubiquitous that many people are not even aware that they are Steinberg inventions. A brief description of these terms and technologies will help you understand them in the context of the software.

ASIO

ASIO stands for Audio Stream Input/Output. Steinberg developed ASIO in order to improve latency issues when recording on a Windows-based computer. Latency is the delay that occurs when audio passes through the computer's operating system into Cubase, and then back out again. This delay can make it difficult to play in time with recorded tracks when overdubbing new tracks in a project. ASIO, which works via a driver installed in the computer, bypasses the normal audio path in the Windows operating system, creating a direct audio path between your audio interface hardware and Cubase. This reduces the latency to as low as 1 millisecond (ms), depending on the computer being used. A delay of less than 6 ms is imperceptible and allows musicians to play in time with recorded tracks while monitoring their signal through Cubase.

ASIO offers other advantages as an audio protocol, including support for multichannel simultaneous recording, support for various bit depths and sample rates, and synchronization between audio devices and video devices.

From the time the company brought it to market, ASIO has been made freely available to third-party software developers with no license fee. This made it easy for audio interface manufacturers to write specific ASIO drivers for their hardware, greatly improving performance and allowing ASIO to become one of the most common audio driver standards in the industry today.

VST

Another major industry standard developed by Steinberg is VST, or Virtual Studio Technology. As its name suggests, Virtual Studio Technology brings the world of the recording studio into the virtual world of the computer. VST brings together a virtual recorder and a virtual mixer, as well as racks of virtual FX and virtual instruments, connecting them inside the computer with no wires or cabling. Steinberg was the first to bring these components together in a user interface that mimics the familiar analog recording studio so the virtual mixer looks like an outboard mixer, virtual effects are kept in a virtual rack and connected through virtual buses, just like outboard gear in the analog world, and so on. This breakthrough made the transition to computer recording easy and comfortable for musicians, and continues to help make recording programs easier to learn.

VSTi

VSTi refers to software instruments using Virtual Studio Technology. The license-free technology of VST has led to an explosion of third-party virtual instruments over the years.

Beats and Loops

2

Cubase is not only a very powerful program for creating and producing music, but is also very flexible in the way it can be used to create different types of music. As you'll see from the variety of professionals featured in the second half of this book, different features are relied upon as essential tools to create different types of music. The features themselves may also be used in different ways for different results.

In this chapter, we'll look at the new features in Cubase 5 that deal with beats and loops. Cubase has enjoyed great success in loop-based music production over the past decade. Features like the Arranger and Play Order Track, Time Warp, and MediaBay have made it easy for musicians, DJs, and producers to create dance, electronic, and urban music, as well as to produce remixes.

The number of VST instruments (VSTi's) included in Cubase grows with every release. Cubase 4 saw the introduction of several new VSTi's and more than 30 new VST plug-ins. There is a very powerful group of onboard synthesizer VSTi's in Prologue, Spector, Mystic, Monologue, and Embracer, as well as HALion One, a sample-playback engine. Cubase 5 adds several rhythm and beat creation VSTi's to its mix of included plug-ins. These include LoopMash, Groove Agent One, and Beat Designer.

LOOPMASH

With the advent of audio sampling, digital video, and computers, mashups have become an integral part of modern culture. You often see mashups as expressions of art, used for entertainment, and even for news and documentaries. A mashup basically takes parts of many different works of audio or video, or both, and weaves them together to produce a new work or variation. What makes a mashup interesting is the way or ways the parts are woven together. There can be a certain intended outcome, or one based entirely on random chance.

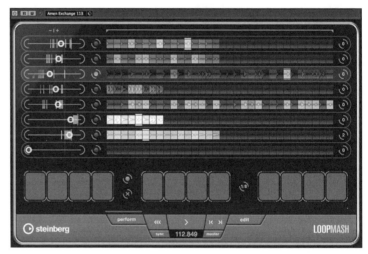

Fig. 2.1: LoopMash

LoopMash (see Fig. 2.1) is based on a brand-new technology originally created by Yamaha that was further developed by Steinberg and incorporated into Cubase 5 as a VST instrument plug-in. The basic idea of LoopMash is to create entirely new loops from existing loops by creating an audio mashup. LoopMash does this by analyzing loops and slicing them to correspond to the beat or tempo. From there, a master loop is selected as the rhythmic base, while slices from other loops are exchanged with slices from the master loop to create an entirely new loop.

Mashing loops together to get new loops may sound simple, but the underlying technology is quite complex. When a loop is imported or dragged into LoopMash, it is analyzed in two ways. First LoopMash determines a number of attributes for the given loop, such as its tempo, rhythm, spectrum, timbre, and more. Second, it slices the loop into eighth-note segments. Once LoopMash has this information about the loop or loops (up to eight can be imported at any one time), it can use it to combine loops, or slices of loops, that have similar attributes to form variations of the master loop, or an entirely new loop, depending on how the parameters are set.

TIP

LoopMash is not only a new technology, but also a new way of working. Most of the time when working with Cubase, you are in control. You determine what edits to make to a vocal track. You determine what sounds and notes of a virtual instrument to play. With LoopMash, however, you give up a bit of control in order to have a more random result. This kind of creative process is not for everyone. Many people want to control the creative process down to the smallest detail, and that's okay. Just keep in mind that while you choose the loops and set a few parameters, the outcome can be something you might not expect.

Getting Around LoopMash

LoopMash is integrated into Cubase 5 as a VST instrument plug-in and is accessed by opening an instrument track, selecting LoopMash from the Synth menu, and designating it as the output. Once LoopMash is open, you'll see eight horizontal lanes on the top two-thirds of the interface, and a series of pads and controls on the bottom third. LoopMash comes with a set of presets, which is a great way to get acquainted with the plug-in. Load a preset by clicking the small diamond next to the name field on the top left of the interface. Once loaded, you'll see the lanes populate with analyzed and sliced audio loops. You can also drag in your own loops to be analyzed and sliced.

LoopMash can hold up to eight loops at a time, and each loop can be sliced into 32 segments. Shorter loops will be repeated, and LoopMash will only use the first 32 slices of longer loops. Highlighting the circle to the left of a loop designates it as the master loop. The bracket across the top of the loop lanes determines the length of the master loop. By changing the master loop, you are changing the loop that will be used as the rhythmic basis. You can hear a slice by clicking on it, even during playback. You can remove a loop by right-clicking or Control-clicking on it. You can transpose a loop by clicking on the icon in brackets to the right of the loop and setting its transposition value from −12 to +12 steps.

You'll notice that the loops and the slices within them appear in various colors. There is more to this than just eye candy, as the colors can help you to quickly identify how each loop and slice is being utilized in LoopMash. While each loop has its own color to allow you to quickly tell them apart, the slices within each loop have varying levels of brightness, depending on how similar their attributes are to the master loop. As LoopMash plays through each slice of the master loop, it analyzes every other slice and readjusts the brightness accordingly. The slice that is selected for playback is highlighted, with white lines above and below it. This process can seem fast to begin with, but after a while you'll begin to see the patterns of similarity between loops and make a connection between what you hear and what you see.

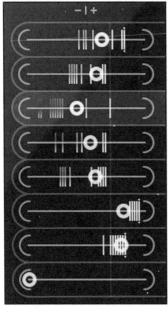

Fig. 2.2: The LoopMash sliders

Another indicator of how LoopMash has analyzed the slices lies in the sliders to the left of each loop (see Fig. 2.2). The vertical lines behind each slider represent the slices of the loop, and how similar or dissimilar each slice is to the master loop slice being played. Similar slices are brighter and appear to the right, while dissimilar slices are darker and appear to the left. If you move the slider to the right, LoopMash will give that loop's similar slices a higher priority upon playback, so you have some control over shaping the outcome of the mashup. Note the faint vertical line going through the sliders about two-thirds of the way to the right. A slice must fall to the right of this line in order for LoopMash to consider it for playback.

The control section found at the bottom of LoopMash (see Fig. 2.3) provides more ways to manipulate the outcome of a mashup. The control section is made up of a transport control, a performance mode, and an edit mode. Standard transport functions are found here, along with a Sync button, which will synchronize the playback tempo of LoopMash with the current Cubase project, and a Master button, which will insert the tempo of the master loop for playback. The Perform button is the default view and shows the scene pads for real-time arranging of loop variations. By clicking the Edit button, you enter Edit mode and the pads are replaced by a series of parameter settings.

Fig 2.3: LoopMash control section

Edit Mode

Along with the "similarity" sliders mentioned above, the parameter settings in Edit mode (see Fig 2.4) allow you to further tailor how LoopMash deals with loops and slices. The first two controls let you select the number of voices, or slices, that will be used to replace the master slice at any given time and the number of slices that can be selected from a single loop. You can select one to four voices for each track. Of course, the more slices you allow from a single loop, the less variety the new loop will have, but this may be what you want.

Fig. 2.4: LoopMash in Edit mode

The next two parameters control slice selection. Slice Selection Offset controls the amount of similarity slices must have to be selected. Move the slider to the right to allow less similar slices to be selected and add more possibilities to the outcome. This is different from the "similarity" sliders mentioned earlier in that it controls all loops in the current scene. Think of it as the master slider, and use the others to fine-tune similarity selection. Random Slice Selection also affects all the slices in the scene, and as the name suggests, it offers more random variation to the slice selection as you move it to the right.

Slice Quantize aligns all slices to the eighth-note grid and in line with the rhythm of the master loop. Staccato Amount will chop each slice as you move it to the right to add a "gated" effect to the overall loop. These two controls can greatly change the feel of the loop, and you should experiment until you get the feel you're after.

The last two parameters in Edit mode are Slice Timestretch and Dry/Wet Mix. Slice Timestretch is applied when you use loops with considerably different original tempos. When activated, it will fill any gaps or tighten any overlaps among loop slices. Steinberg cautions that using Slice Timestretch will increase the CPU usage and affect the sound quality, so you may want to use loops that have similar tempos. Dry/Wet Mix is simply the balance between the amount of the master loop and the selected slices that you hear on playback.

Performance Mode

In Performance mode, the default view, entered from Edit mode by clicking the Perform button, LoopMash uses 12 pads to store configurations and settings for later recall (see Fig. 2.5). Each pad holds a "scene": eight loops and all of their parameter settings. Each scene can use different loops, so it's possible for LoopMash to hold up to 96 loops in one instance. Empty pads will appear black, pads with saved scenes will appear gray, and the current loaded scene will appear white.

Fig. 2.5: LoopMash in Performance mode

TIP

Save your current scene to a pad before selecting another pad; otherwise any parameter changes you had made will be lost.

After the first four pads, you'll see an orange circle and an X. To save the current scene to a pad, click the circle and then click on a pad. To delete a scene, click on the X and then click the pad of the scene you want to delete. After the next four pads there is a control that lets you select when LoopMash will change to the next scene. You may want to change this if you're using LoopMash live versus simply auditioning scenes.

TIP

Using LoopMash on stage with a MIDI keyboard is easy. The pads in LoopMash are mapped from left to right to MIDI notes C through B, allowing you to change scenes from a MIDI keyboard in real time.

Finally, once you have all the scenes set up and saved the way you want them, you can save the entire LoopMash instance as a VST preset. Simply click the icon in the Preset field at the top of the interface and select Save Preset. Choose a name and tag the preset for easier recall in the MediaBay.

INSIDER
Steinberg Senior Product Planning Manager
Arnd Kaiser on LoopMash

"LoopMash is something that I'm personally very proud of, because it's a totally new technology and something that has never been done before. We first heard about it three years ago from Yamaha, which spent a lot of resources on research, working with universities across the globe researching new sound and audio technologies. They showed it to us, and from the very beginning I wanted to have it in Cubase. We decided to do it as a virtual instrument to keep it contained, because it's so different from everything else that people are used to. In Cubase, you would expect to have full control, but the idea of LoopMash is to let go of some of the control and let it be part of the creative process by suggesting ideas. So you can combine loops, and LoopMash will replace slices with slices from other loops, and what you get is something like an audio mosaic. You know those mosaics where you take photos of people and put them together as a collage and then you zoom out and it becomes another picture? This is basically the way that LoopMash works with audio: instead of looking at individual loops, it mashes them into something completely new."

GROOVE AGENT ONE

Groove Agent One is a sample-based drum machine that is triggered from a MIDI track in Cubase or from a MIDI keyboard. It's a logical assumption to think that Groove Agent One is simply a scaled-down version of Steinberg's Groove Agent 3 Virtual Drummer VSTi, which is sold separately, but its intent is a bit different. Groove Agent 3 is designed to give you automatic drum or rhythm parts based on prerecorded performances and parameter settings. The idea is to hit Play and tweak sliders, knobs, and faders until you get the grooves and sounds that you want. Groove Agent One is an MPC-style drum machine with 16 pads for playback and editing. There are no prerecorded tracks here; you need to supply your own via a MIDI file, MIDI keyboard, or the new Beat Designer built into Cubase 5 (more on that in the next section). I wouldn't call Groove Agent One a light version of Groove Agent 3. In some ways, it's actually more powerful. It really depends on what you want, as they are designed for different purposes.

When you first open Groove Agent One on an instrument track, you'll immediately notice its MPC styling (see Fig. 2.6). The interface is divided in halves, with a large virtual LCD display and a number of knobs, buttons, and a slider below on the left half and 16 pads and a row of buttons on the right half.

Fig. 2.6: Groove Agent One

Getting Around Groove Agent One

I'll start with the pads, since they dominate the work surface of the interface. Each pad contains the MIDI note it's mapped to and the name of the sample it's playing back (see Fig. 2.7). They light up orange when played and green during editing. While you can only see 16 pads on the screen, they are organized into eight groups for a total of 128 pads, or one for every available MIDI note. You'll know a group has samples assigned to pads if the group number has a glowing red ring around it.

Assigning a sample to a pad is as simple as dragging an audio sample onto it from the MediaBay or from the Project window. You can also drag and drop from pad to pad and group to group. You can assign up to eight samples to a pad, which will show up as layers. Clicking a pad at the bottom plays the sample back at a low velocity or softly, while clicking at the top plays it back at a high velocity, or loudly. To remove a sample from a pad, click the pad and drag it to the trash icon in Groove Agent One's LCD display. To rename a pad, simply right/Control-click it, and to mute it, just Shift-click it. You can layer samples by dragging up to eight onto one pad.

Fig. 2.7: Groove Agent One pads and groups

POWER TIP
Velocity Switching for Added Snare Drum Realism

As the centerpiece of the drum kit, the snare drum is often struck many different ways to produce different sounds. Multiple samples assigned to one pad of Groove Agent One can be assigned different playback velocities to simulate a real player. This can be useful for adding realism to a drum track.

1. Assign or drag three different snare samples to the same pad: a light snare hit, a medium snare hit, and a hard snare hit.

2. Go to the Voice, Filter, or Amplifier Edit page and go to the Layer Bar toward the top of the LCD.

3. Adjust the velocity range of each layer by placing your mouse over the lines between layers, and dragging left or right. You can do this for up to eight samples per pad for very intricate velocity switching.

Fig. 2.8: The Groove Agent One
Edit section

Editing

Once your samples are assigned to pads, you can edit them in a number of ways to fine-tune them or create entirely new sounds. The editing controls are found beneath the LCD display (see Fig. 2.8). The six knobs correspond to the parameters displayed above them in the LCD. In the Pad Edit section there are four pages: Play, Voice, Filter, and Amplifier. For each of these pages, you will see information about the samples in the LCD as well as the parameters that can be adjusted to tailor your sounds.

The Play page is a "master page" of sorts. The LCD screen displays some general information about the current kit and some of the most common parameters for a selected pad: volume, pan, coarse tuning, cutoff frequency, Q or resonance, and output. All of these parameter controls are repeated at various places in the Voice, Filter, and Amplifier pages, but are listed here for quick adjustments. You can adjust parameters by clicking on a value and typing in a change, or by simply turning the knob below it.

For more detailed editing, you can go to the other three pages in the Pad Edit section. The Voice page offers access to parameters related to the sample itself: reverse mode, coarse and fine-tuning, mute group, one-shot, and output. The Filter page contains parameters related to processing the sample: filter type, cut-off frequency, Q or resonance, and modulation velocity. The Amplifier page contains volume, pan, attack time, release time, amplifier modulation, and attack modulation. By experimenting with these editing pages, you can tweak your samples and kits to your liking or even come up with entirely new-sounding kits.

POWER TIP
Use Mute Group in the Voice Page for Realistic Hi-Hat Lines

When a drummer plays an open hi-hat, it is naturally cut off when he or she lowers their foot, producing a closed "clamp" sound. You can create this effect with Groove Agent One mute groups.

1. Assign or drag a closed hi-hat sample to one pad, an open hi-hat sound to another, and a "foot" hi-hat sample to a third pad.

2. Click on the closed hi-hat pad and go to the Voice Edit page.

3. On the LCD screen, locate the Mute Group tab, click it, and assign the pad to group 1.

4. Repeat step 3 for the open hi-hat pad and the "foot" hi-hat pad.

5. Now, playing one of these samples will cut off any of the others that were played before it, resulting in a naturally played hi-hat part.

Besides telling you what parameters you are adjusting on a given page, the LCD screen indicates some other useful things. On the Play page, it tells you how many pads are used in a kit, how many samples those pads hold, the overall size (in MB) the kit is, and the polyphony. On the Voice, Filter, and Amplifier pages, the LCD shows the sample name and MIDI note, a trash icon (for removing samples from pads), a MIDI input on/off icon, layer selection, parameter values, and a waveform representation of the sample. Finally, if you look closely, you will see a small slider on the top of the LCD that controls the brightness, just like a hardware LCD on a drum machine.

TIP

While pads can hold multiple samples that can be velocity switched, sample layers cannot be edited individually. Adjusting parameters in the Edit pages will affect all layers on a given pad.

Fig. 2.9: Groove Agent One Global section

Global

In the upper right corner of the Groove Agent One interface, you'll see a small section labeled "Global" (see Fig. 2.9). By engaging the V-Max button here, all samples in the current kit will play back at maximum velocity. Clicking the Reset button will clear all samples from all pads in the current kit. To engage the Reset button, you must hold down the Shift key while clicking it, then click again to clear all samples. This is simply a safety precaution against an accidental reset.

To the right of the Pad Edit section and the Master Output fader is a section labeled Exchange (see Fig. 2.10). This is for

Fig. 2.10: Groove Agent One Exchange section

importing Akai MPC files (.pgm) and exporting MIDI files (see the Power Tip below).

POWER TIP
Triggering a Sliced Loop with Groove Agent
One Using MIDI

Groove Agent One allows you to drag and drop several files, which it will automatically map to separate pads. This allows you to trigger a sliced-up loop from a MIDI keyboard or drum controller in real time for live performance or for playing new grooves using the sounds from your favorite audio loops.

1. Load your audio loop into the Project and open it in the Sample Editor.
2. In the Inspector, open the Hitpoints tab and select the Slice & Close function.
3. Click and drag the sliced audio loop onto an empty pad in Groove Agent One.
4. Groove Agent One will map the slices to individual pads.
5. Click the MIDI icon in the upper right corner of the LCD display in the Voice, Filter, or Amplifier Edit pages so it is highlighted.

You can now trigger the individual sounds from your loop via MIDI. If a pad is already assigned, Groove Agent One will find another available pad, even if it's in another bank, so I recommend using an empty Groove Agent One instance to be sure to get all the slices mapped in a logical order. Also, the pads will all have the same name, which is the name of the original audio loop, so you'll need to go through and rename each slice/pad.

POWER TIP
Creating a MIDI File from an Audio Loop with
Groove Agent One

When importing the sliced-up audio loop, Groove Agent One creates a MIDI file that contains the original groove of the audio loop. You can use this MIDI file to further edit the audio loop. Instead of one continuous audio loop, you now have a MIDI file that triggers the samples used in the original loop.

1. Click and hold on the double arrow in the Exchange section of the interface (after importing the sliced audio it should be highlighted).
2. Drag to a MIDI track in the Project window.
3. The MIDI file that Groove Agent One created from the audio loop will appear.

If you want to use the sounds from the original audio loop, simply place the MIDI file in the Groove Agent One instrument track. You can also place it on any other MIDI or instrument track to play back different sounds with the original groove.

BEAT DESIGNER

Beat Designer is one of the new creative tools in Cubase 5 and, as its name suggests, it is primarily designed to create beats, or drum tracks. Beat Designer is a MIDI plug-in and works as a MIDI insert on a virtual instrument track. When it is matched with percussive content it can help you come up with drum tracks, percussion tracks, techno beats, dance rhythms, and so on. When it is matched with pitched percussive or even nonpercussive content, Beat Designer can be a unique creative tool for rhythmic sound design. Experimentation is the key here. Rather than having a concrete beat or musical idea in your head, Beat Designer lets you place notes along a looped step sequencer and experiment with these placements and sounds until you get what you want (or better yet, something completely new you hadn't even thought of).

Beat Designer is like an extension of the Drum Editor in Cubase. It is similar in many ways, but more creative. The Drum Editor is not meant to be a creative tool, but an editing tool for a performance that has already been recorded or programmed. The Drum Editor lays out drum sounds corresponding to piano key pitches positioned vertically along the left side of the screen.

As the timeline of bars and beats scrolls across the top from left to right, the notes of the MIDI part that correspond to a particular sound appear in, or can be placed, in the field to the right, while velocities appear across the bottom. While this is a great way to edit a performance that's already recorded, it's not a very easy way to create a performance from scratch.

Beat Designer has many elements that are similar to the Drum Editor: notes or sounds are shown vertically along the left side, the timeline moves from left to right, there is a field for entering and editing notes, and a way to edit velocity. But instead of depicting a linear timeline of bars and beats that progress through the entire piece of music, Beat Designer is based on patterns, making it much faster to create and edit parts in real time.

Getting Around Beat Designer

The user interface centers around an eight-lane, 16-step sequencer that loops and is synced with the tempo of the current Cubase project (see Fig. 2.11). In the adjustment bar in the upper left you will see a pull-down arrow that contains general tools such as Shift Left and Right, Reverse, Copy, Paste, and Clear Pattern; several Insert options; and a Fill Loop with Pattern command. Continuing across the top bar, you can set the number of steps from 1 to 64, adjust the step resolution, give it a name, and enter Jump mode, which we'll get to later.

Fig. 2.11: Beat Designer

The left-hand column of the interface shows the instrument name and its corresponding MIDI note on the piano keyboard. Clicking on an instrument name pulls up a menu of the sounds available from the MIDI instrument. To the left of each instrument name is a speaker icon, which auditions a sound when clicked, and to the right of each name are mute and solo buttons. The step sequencer field dominates the middle portion of the interface.

To use Beat Designer, you first match it with a MIDI instrument, the default being Cubase 5's built-in Groove Agent One Virtual Drummer, press Play, and start adding notes to the step sequencer field by clicking them into place. Clicking and dragging on a note allows you to change the velocity from zero to 127. Clicking and dragging from left to right over the notes in a lane will allow you to draw a velocity curve across several notes. Holding down Shift and adjusting the velocity of one note will simultaneously adjust the velocities of all notes in that lane. Clicking on a note will simply remove it.

POWER TIP
Save Time by Knowing Where to Click

You can save some time editing velocity by clicking notes into the step sequencer at three different MIDI velocities.

1. To have a note play back loudly (MIDI velocity 110), click the note into place while holding the mouse over the top third of the note area.

2. To have a note play back at medium volume (MIDI velocity 80), click the note into place holding the mouse over the middle third of the note area.

3. To have a note play back softly (MIDI velocity of 50), click the note into place holding the mouse over the bottom third of the note area.

By entering notes at various levels, you can quickly get a feel for the dynamics of a beat and make any fine adjustments needed later. To give you a visual cue, soft notes appear red, medium notes orange, and loud notes appear yellow. This may seem backwards and you might expect red notes to be loudest, but

Steinberg explained to me that it was done this way to mimic a candle flame, where the hottest part of the flame, the center, is yellow, the middle part orange, and the outer, or coolest part of the flame is red. OK, this seems a bit unrelated to music, but you get used to it after working with Beat Designer for a while.

Flams

Fig. 2.12: Flams created on a note

Fig. 2.13: Sliders for adjusting flam settings

Steinberg has done a good job of packing a lot of power into a very clean user interface. One of the ways it does this is by allowing some of the editing to be done within each Beat Designer note. It's not apparent when you first see them, but those orange, red, and yellow rectangles hold some secrets. Along with being able to adjust velocity by clicking, holding, and dragging, hovering your mouse over the bottom portion of a note reveals three small circles. These circles represent flams. Clicking on the first circle creates a single-stroke flam. Clicking on the second circle creates a double-stroke flam. Clicking on the third circle creates a triple-stroke flam (see Fig. 2.12). Once you have created a single-, double-, or triple-stroke flam, you can edit it using the sliders on the lower left of the interface. Here you will find three rows of circles; one, two, and three, flanked by three horizontal sliders to the left and three vertical sliders to the right (see Fig. 2.13). The three horizontal sliders to the left represent the three strokes of the flam in relation to the beat. Placing the slider on the middle line will place the corresponding flam stroke directly on the beat. Moving the slider to the left places the flam stroke ahead of the beat, and moving it to the right places it behind the beat. The three vertical sliders to the right of the circles represent the velocity of each flam stroke. Because the timing of MIDI data is somewhat complicated, many programs don't have this level of editing when it comes to flams, especially the ability to place a flam ahead of the beat, which is where it is naturally played. It may seem like a small thing, but good flams can add a lot of dimension to a rhythm part.

Swing and Slide

On the right side of the screen, you will find a column of horizontal sliders with single and double slash marks to the left of them and plus and minus signs to the right (see Fig 2.14). This is where Beat Designer deals with Swing and Slide in the program. Each slider corresponds to an instrument row and allows you to adjust the Slide for each instrument. As you move the slider to the left, all the notes for that instrument row will move ahead of the beat, whereas moving the slider to the right will move the notes after or behind the beat. You can select one of two Swing settings for each instrument by clicking on the single or double slash mark. Leave them blank to have the instrument play back completely straight. You can then adjust the amount of swing for each instrument by moving the master slider at the bottom of the column that corresponds with the single or double slash mark you selected. (The small + and – signs to the right of the sliders allow you to add or remove an instrument lane and have nothing to do with swing or slide.) The combination of two independent Swing and Slide controls per instrument is not only very powerful, but makes dialing in the right feel very fast and easy.

Banks and Patterns

Turning your attention to the bottom part of the interface, you will find a one-octave virtual piano keyboard and bars labeled 1, 2, 3, and 4 above it (see Fig. 2.15). This is where patterns and sub-banks are stored. When a pattern is entered, a small circle appears on the note and in its corresponding sub-bank to let you easily track where your content is. Each note on the virtual keyboard can hold a pattern within four sub-banks, giving you a possible 48 patterns. If this is not enough, you can always open another instance of Beat Designer on a different track within Cubase. And because it's a MIDI plug-in and its CPU usage is very low, there shouldn't be many limitations to opening as many instances as you need.

So now that we've looked at the interface and know how to enter notes and create patterns, how do we switch patterns to form an arrangement? There are a few ways to do this. The easiest way is to simply click the bank number and virtual keyboard note you want to hear while Beat Designer is playing in real time. While this can be fun, help you get ideas, and maybe be used in a live scenario, it's not the most practical method. The second way is to drag a pattern from the Beat Designer's virtual keyboard to

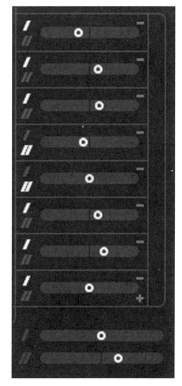

Fig. 2.14: Sliders to adjust swing and slide

Fig. 2.15: Beat Designer's keyboard stores banks and patterns

an empty MIDI or instrument track in the Project Window and then turn Beat Designer off. This is a great way to get patterns out of Beat Designer and convert them into standard MIDI tracks for playback, arranging, and editing in traditional ways with the Drum, Key, Score, or List Editors. However, once you move a pattern out of Beat Designer, you cannot move it back in for further editing. In order to arrange your pattern within a project and keep it stored within Beat Designer, Steinberg created Jump mode. Jump mode lets you trigger patterns within Beat Designer by pressing a note on a MIDI keyboard or by pressing a pattern key on the virtual keyboard and recording it into the project track. This places a program change in the timeline and tells Beat Designer what pattern to change to when in your arrangement. The big advantage of this is that you can keep your patterns within Beat Designer for organization as well as recall them for further editing, the Beat Designer way, anytime down the road. If you want to "play" an arrangement live, Jump mode is the best method, as you can trigger patterns from a MIDI keyboard, a very natural way to perform.

POWER TIP
Beat Designer Key Command Shortcuts

1. Move all the steps in a lane together: Shift and drag left or right.
2. Invert a lane: Press Alt/Option and drag the mouse over the lane.
3. Copy a lane: Press Alt/Option while clicking to the left of the lane you want to copy, and drag to a new lane.
4. Copy a pattern: Ctrl/Command+C.
5. Paste a pattern: Ctrl/Command+V.

INSIDER
Steinberg Software Developer Paul Grathwohl on the Challenges of Developing Beat Designer

"Developing Beat Designer's Jump mode was quite tricky. In this mode, you can trigger the patterns by pressing a key on a MIDI keyboard or by pressing a pattern button in Beat Designer. This works in relation to the project timeline in Cubase, and there are certain internal things which make this difficult, because MIDI is always processed before audio. So, if you want to change the pattern in real time, some MIDI notes may have already gone out to the playback device, and it's not really possible to get them back. There was quite a bit of analysis and testing that went into making this work correctly.

Another area that takes great care is the integration of a plug-in like Beat Designer into Cubase. It's not only a matter of making Beat Designer work within itself, but there are many things outside of the plug-in that we must consider. For example, Beat Designer supports pattern banks in MediaBay, which we must consider when thinking about how the patterns and banks work within the plug-in as well as how to save and load presets."

Vocal and Pitch Editing

3

It's little argued that in most genres of music, the vocal is the most important part of a song. In music that has no vocals, many times there is a solo instrument line playing a melody or theme that functions the same way as a vocal line. Many products over the years have focused on vocal or monophonic editing and pitch correction, from stand-alone hardware boxes to software plug-ins. But vocal editing is one area that has traditionally been lacking in the tools built into DAWs.

Cubase 5 includes two new tools dedicated to vocal editing and pitch correction: VariAudio and PitchCorrect. These two tools, while focusing on the same area of production, function differently and are intended for different purposes: in-depth vocal editing or quick, automatic pitch correction in real time.

VARIAUDIO

VariAudio is designed for editing the pitch and timing of monophonic musical lines, mainly to fix pitch, intonation, and timing problems on vocal tracks. VariAudio evolved from the development of AudioWarp, which first appeared in Cubase SX3 (see Fig. 3.1). AudioWarp was limited to time stretching in that version, and Steinberg developed it further with a "transpose" function for pitch shifting in Cubase 4. In Cubase 5, VariAudio builds on its predecessors and is much more effective at analyzing and editing vocal lines in real time to solve intonation and timing problems, and can even be used creatively to alter vocal lines and create harmonies.

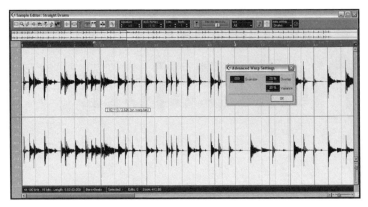

Fig. 3.1: AudioWarp from Cubase SX3

Because VariAudio is built directly into the Sample Editor in Cubase 5, it feels like part of the program instead of just an effects plug-in (see Fig. 3.2). I asked Steinberg development about the decision to place VariAudio in the Sample Editor instead of selling it as a separate plug-in like Celemony's Melodyne. The answer was twofold. First, and probably most important, by building VariAudio into Cubase 5 as an editor, the audio that is being edited never leaves the program. This is important in keeping the edit and undo history intact and the editing process nondestructive. Once the audio leaves Cubase and enters a plug-in or stand-alone program, Cubase no longer sees it. The edited audio needs to be brought back in to the project at some point, and the edits then cannot be undone and the original file is lost. Another reason was to give you a consistent workflow: you already know how to use the Sample Editor; therefore you know how to use VariAudio. It works very much the same way, so you don't have to learn a new system. The second reason VariAudio is not sold separately is more of a marketing issue. Steinberg greatly believes in creating a valuable package that allows you to do complete music production under one roof. In the past, the conventional wisdom was to make the main program a recorder and sell everything else—effects, instruments, and editors—as add-ons. Now, most companies include a comprehensive set of tools inside the main software package to give you a better value.

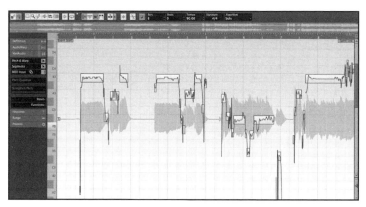

Fig. 3.2: VariAudio

Getting Around VariAudio

As you would expect, you access VariAudio through the Sample Editor. Double-clicking the audio event in the Project window opens the Sample Editor. From there, select the VariAudio tab in the Inspector and highlight the Pitch & Warp arrow to analyze the audio. The waveform is displayed in the familiar left-to-right manner in the timeline. However, once the vocal line is analyzed, the waveform becomes watermarked in the background as a timing reference, and the individual notes of the melody line appear over the top of it in the form of colored blocks. The notes align with a virtual keyboard shown along the left for pitch reference. Within each note, and in between them, curved lines follow micro-pitches that bend and nonpitched transitions from one note to the next.

TIP

It's a good idea to use VariAudio last in editing a vocal track, as applying any offline processes normally done in the Sample Editor, or making any edits to the original audio file, will undo or invalidate the edits done in VariAudio. The reason for this is that certain processes require Cubase to reanalyze the audio file. To avoid this, do things like applying fades, normalizing, editing the file length, or applying effects to the track first, then do your edits in VariAudio.

Segmentation

Sometimes you may want to change the way VariAudio segments your vocal track or the way it analyzes the audio and puts the notes into blocks for editing. There may be times when you want to move the consonant sound, represented as the lines between the note blocks, with a pitched note block so that it sounds more natural. To do this, go to the Inspector under the VariAudio tab and highlight the arrow next to Segments to enter Segment mode (see Fig. 3.3). You'll notice that the note blocks now have a hatched background. In this mode, you edit notes the same way you did in Pitch & Warp mode, but the results will be different. As you hold the mouse over the sides of a segment, a double arrow will appear. Click and drag to change the length of a segment, which may include a transition if you need one. Hover your mouse over the top to move the segment to the left or right. Hover over the bottom and a scissors tool will appear so you can split the segment into two, or you can hold down Alt/ Option to glue segments together.

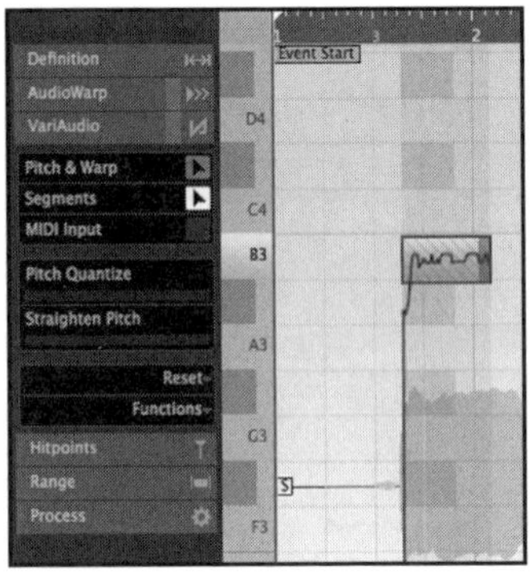

Fig. 3.3: VariAudio Segments tab

TIP

You should make any changes to the segmentation first before editing pitch and timing. VariAudio will need to recalculate the file after resegmenting, and any changes in pitch will be lost. When VariAudio initially analyzes the audio file, listen and look at the resulting note blocks, searching for any areas where you anticipate changing the pitch. In these areas, determine if the transitions should be a part of the note you will move or if they can remain in place. This takes a little foresight, but is well worth it in the final result.

Editing Pitch

Now that you have an analyzed vocal line that is graphically segmented the way you want, you can edit the notes in pitch and in time. Make sure you are in Pitch & Warp mode by highlighting the arrow next to these words in the Inspector (see Fig. 3.4). Clicking on a note will play it and also place the virtual keyboard behind it as a watermark. This gives you two frames of reference for pitch. A third pitch reference, note name and cent steps, can be obtained by zooming in on a note segment. Meanwhile, you can still see the waveform in the background and its position on the timeline for two time references. Editing pitch is as simple as hovering the mouse over a note until the hand appears, clicking and holding, then dragging it up or down. As you move the note, you will hear it played at its new pitch.

Fig. 3.4: VariAudio Pitch & Warp tab

To speed the pitch-editing process, you can quantize the audio to the nearest semitone on the virtual keyboard. This can be done in various degrees to place pitches directly on the notes, or to move them closer to the notes in a more subtle way. To do this, select the segments you want to quantize: a single note or the whole track. Move the Pitch Quantize slider in the Inspector to adjust the amount of quantization.

Many times, intonation problems can happen within one note, such as when a singer holds a note at the end of a phrase and it falls flat as they run out of breath. Rather than move the entire note segment in VariAudio, you can adjust the micro-pitch within it in one of two ways. The first way is by "tilting" the note (see Fig. 3.5). To do this, hold the mouse over the upper right or upper left end of a segment until a vertical double arrow appears. Click and drag this arrow to pull the ends of the pitch up or down. You can fine-tune the part of the pitch to pull by clicking an anchor point into the line that appears across the top of the note segment. Only the part of the pitch on either side of the anchor point will now be pulled.

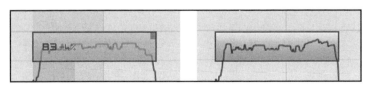

Fig. 3.5: VariAudio Tilt before and after

The second way to correct intonation problems is by straightening the pitch within a note segment. Doing this is as simple as selecting a note segment or segments and adjusting the Straighten Pitch slider in the Inspector to the desired amount (see Fig. 3.6). Be careful, though, as too much of this will make the transitions between notes choppy and the notes themselves very static. The result will sound very robotic, like the now-famous "Cher" effect.

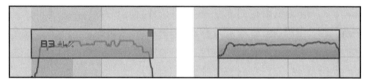

Fig. 3.6: VariAudio Straighten Pitch before and after

You can also change pitches in VariAudio by using a MIDI keyboard if you prefer to relate pitch editing to a piano keyboard, and the onscreen virtual version isn't to your liking. To do this, simply select the note segment you want to change and click MIDI Input in the Inspector. Then simply play a note on your MIDI keyboard, and the segment will change to that note. This is called Still mode—editing one note at a time. There is another mode called Step mode. Enter this mode by holding Alt or Option (Mac) and clicking MIDI Input. Now when you change the segment selected by playing a note on your MIDI keyboard, VariAudio will automatically select the next segment, so you can play the entire melody line while editing the pitch to match.

POWER TIP
Creating a Harmony with VariAudio

While VariAudio is in its first generation and doesn't include automatic harmony creation, you can still create simple harmonies quickly and with good results.

1. Make a copy of the section of the vocal track that you want to harmonize and place it on an adjacent track.

2. Double-click on the copy to go into the Sample Editor, click on the VariAudio tab, and select Pitch & Warp mode.

3. After VariAudio analyzes and segments the audio, select all the notes.

4. Drag the notes up to the third (the original track will remain at the root).

You now have a simple harmony that is a third higher than the original. Since it is an exact copy of the original, it may sound a bit stiff or unnatural. You can remedy this by altering the harmony to make it a little different than the original. Try applying some straightening to the notes and nudging them ahead or behind the original. This will help lend a more "human" feel to the harmony.

Editing Timing

Editing the timing of notes, or Warping segments, is done in the same screen mode as editing pitch. Hold your mouse over the right or left end of the segment (use the small dots as a guide), and a horizontal double arrow appears. By simply clicking and dragging this arrow, you can adjust the length of the note from the beginning or the end of it without changing the pitch or transitions (see Fig. 3.7). This is different from changing the length of a segment in Segment mode. Here, the audio within the segment will be shortened or lengthened, whereas in Segment mode the audio will not be changed, just the size of the note segment.

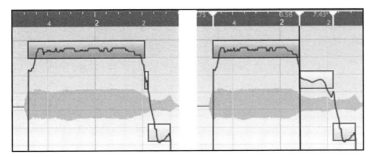

Fig. 3.7: VariAudio warp or timing adjustment before and after

When warping note segments in VariAudio, the warp tabs, the vertical lines that extend all the way up into the timeline, are not in any way associated with the project tempo in Cubase. They are instead aligned with the note segments of the vocal track. If you need or would like to reference the tabs to the project tempo, go into the AudioWarp tab in the Inspector and turn on Musical mode by highlighting the quarter note in the square. Then, when you return to VariAudio, you'll notice warp tabs in the timeline that correspond to the project tempo. Dragging these tabs to a note segment will adjust that segment to the nearest beat. This works well if you need certain words or pitches to hit directly on a particular beat.

Extracting MIDI from Audio

VariAudio also lets you extract MIDI from an audio track to create an identical MIDI part that is placed on a MIDI track and played back via a VST instrument or external MIDI device. To do this, simply click on the Functions tab in the VariAudio Inspector and select Extract MIDI. You can then select what mode you want to extract the MIDI data: just notes and no pitch-bend data, notes and static pitch-bend data, or notes and continuous pitch-bend data. You then select the pitch-bend range and the destination for the new MIDI track (see Fig. 3.8).

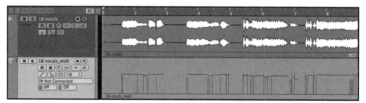

Fig. 3.8: A MIDI track (below) extracted from an audio track (above)

INSIDER
Steinberg Software Developer Klaus Mueller
on the Challenges of Developing VariAudio

"The segmentation was the most difficult part of developing VariAudio. Analyzing the audio and coming out with segmented pieces that accurately represent the notes, while not missing any notes or combining two notes, is a complex process.

Also, to get a smooth transition between the notes is very detailed work. If you have one pitch or note, the natural transition to the next note is smooth. So, if you move a note from one pitch to another, there still has to be a smooth transition from the first note to the next note so it will also sound natural. It needs to be an audible transition and not an instant shift, and it also has to be represented graphically. In the very first version we developed, it was just doing a transposition, and we could hear a hiccup. We needed to separate the tonal part from the noise part. If the singer sings the word 'she,' for example, the 'sh' would be the noise and the 'e' would be the tonal or the pitched part. So we have to make a decision to shift the 'sh' to the next pitch, or leave it with the previous pitch. That was hard to decide. Sometimes it's better to leave it as it is and sometimes you need to shift it. That is all done in the analysis part of the process. Of course, you can change this by editing the segmentation in case VariAudio analyzes the audio differently than you want.

Looking forward, we have lots of ideas, and it's a whole new area. So, for this first step we decided to focus on the most common corrections that people will want to do: intonation and timing correction. At the moment it's monophonic, so if you want another voice for a harmony, for example, you would copy it to another track and then manipulate it from there.

You can push it further than simple correction, of course. You can get the 'Cher' effect going and abuse it if you like. For me as a developer, the creative aspect is the most interesting potential for VariAudio. But from a user perspective, we had to make it really useful to begin with. It is also part of the process of development, where technologies are added to and extended down the line. This is where we are at today, and you may see the culmination of several versions in later updates of Cubase, just as we used to have only AudioWarp and now we have VariAudio."

PITCHCORRECT

While VariAudio is designed to perform more detailed and precise editing of the pitch and timing of vocal and monophonic instrument tracks, PitchCorrect is designed to automatically correct pitch and intonation problems in real time. PitchCorrect comes from the Yamaha-Steinberg relationship, deriving its algorithm from Yamaha's Pitch Fix effects processor, found in products like the AW16 and AW2400 DAWs.

Getting Around PitchCorrect

PitchCorrect is an audio effect plug-in, and is found in the Inspector of an audio track under the Inserts tab. Once you select Pitch Shift–Pitch Correct for your vocal or monophonic instrument track, it will open, and you'll see something that closely resembles a VST instrument (see Fig. 3.9). The interface depicts a piano keyboard across the bottom third, a series of vertical lanes across the middle third that align with the keyboard, and some parameter adjustments across the top. The interface is rather sparse and the controls are few. This is because it's meant to be mostly automatic and must remain spare so it can quickly analyze incoming audio and process it in real time, while keeping CPU resources at reasonable levels.

Fig. 3.9: PitchCorrect interface

After opening PitchCorrect on your track and pushing Play, you'll notice your track streaming through the plug-in in the vertical lanes, each note in blue aligning with its corresponding note on the piano keyboard. PitchCorrect is actually analyzing the audio in much the same way as VariAudio, and you will see variations in the pitch as well as bends and consonants represented by waves, bends, and horizontal lines. You may be a bit thrown off by the audio flying by vertically, but this makes it much easier to see the pitch in relation to the piano keyboard as opposed to a horizontal track with a vertical piano keyboard to the side like in an editor. Keep in mind, you are not editing here, but simply setting some parameters and letting PitchCorrect make the correction automatically.

Parameter Settings

As for the parameters, there are three categories across the top of the interface, labeled Correction, Scale Source, and Formant. In the Correction section, you can adjust the Speed, or sensitivity, of the audio analysis, the Tolerance, how smooth the pitch shift will be, and the Transposition of the audio in half-step increments. In the Scale Source section you can select from the internal source or an external MIDI source. If you select the internal source, you can then select the Major, Minor, or Custom scale, which lets you click the notes you want the audio to correct to. If you select an external MIDI source you can "play" the corrections from your keyboard in real time. The last parameter category is Formant, or the natural timbre of a voice. Here you can Shift to change the formant, Optimize it for male or female voice, or turn Preservation of the formant on and off.

Lastly, there is a master tune control just above the vertical lanes on the right side of the interface. The default tuning is 440 Hz.

T I P

For natural-sounding results, it's important that the formant of a particular voice remain unchanged as the pitch is shifted. Formant is the resonance and other factors that give the human voice "male" or "female" characteristics. Because PitchCorrect gives you the option to change the formant, or shift it with the pitch, you can use it as a vocal effect with extreme settings to make squeaky chipmunk voices or rumbling T-Rex groans. This can be a great tool when doing narration or audio for film or video projects.

Once you have set your parameters and play the audio track through PitchCorrect, the corrected audio will again appear blue in the vertical lanes, while the original audio will appear in orange behind it (see Fig. 3.10). This gives you a visual cue as to the amount of correction that is happening in addition to the audible difference. This comes in handy when you are doing subtle corrections and want to make sure PitchCorrect is engaged and working.

Fig. 3.10: PitchCorrect passing audio and correcting pitch

Creative Control

Aside from performing subtle intonation correction on the fly during a mix, PitchCorrect has some interesting creative uses as well. You can change a line from major to minor, to an entirely different key for remixing or to work out a song arrangement. Using an external MIDI keyboard can make PitchCorrect an interesting tool for live use on stage or for simply making scale changes faster. You could copy the original track to a new track and use PitchCorrect to automatically shift the new track to create a harmony. As with any effect, nothing is off limits. It depends on what you're after, but in the end experimentation is key.

POWER TIP

Changing the Scale in Real Time via a **MIDI** Keyboard

If you prefer to work via a MIDI keyboard, you can quickly change or audition different scales with PitchCorrect.

1. Connect a MIDI keyboard to Cubase.

2. In PitchCorrect, set the Scale Source to External–MIDI Scale.

3. Play a chord on the MIDI keyboard.

4. PitchCorrect will adjust the audio to match the scale of the chord played.

You can play different chords in real time to find the correction that you like. You can also tweak the other parameters inside of PitchCorrect to get the results you're looking for.

Recording and Mixing

4

Since Cubase's early days as purely a MIDI sequencer, it has evolved into one of the most powerful and flexible recorders and mixers to grace a computer screen. In version 5, Steinberg has continued to refine Cubase's recording and mixing functionality, providing new tools in both the audio and MIDI realms. One improvement is Cubase's lane management, which now makes the handling of multiple takes easier and faster. A Lock Record function has been added to prevent missing takes in the studio or live, as well as a Remaining Record Time display so you'll be sure not to run out of hard disk space during a session or gig. Steinberg has even added a virtual MIDI keyboard to the transport bar for those times when you need a quick MIDI input without hooking up outboard gear (see Fig. 4.1).

Fig. 4.1: Virtual MIDI keyboard in the transport bar (left-hand side)

In this chapter, we'll look at REVerence, Steinberg's entry into the world of high-end convolution reverb; two new track types, Signature Track and Tempo Track; and enhancements to the automation handling in Cubase 5, including a new way of working with MIDI automation data.

REVERENCE

Reverb is the most common audio effect in almost any recording, performing, or mixing situation. It's used in every conceivable way, from making tracks sound more natural, adding "meat" to samples, and blending to placing a track in a completely new environment or simply making a singer feel more confident during a tracking session. Reverb has been produced in several ways over the years—echo chambers, reverberating plates and springs, and digital simulations have all been used to great success. More recently, convolution reverb has come into vogue. While the theory behind this technology is quite complex, I will keep it simple for our purposes here.

Convolution reverb is in many ways the best of both the natural, or analog, world and digital technology. Rather than reverberate a real object like a plate or a spring, or digitally simulate reverberation with feedback loops, convolution reverb uses a recorded impulse response of an actual space as the basis of a digital model to create the reverb effect.

An impulse response is the output (response) of a system when input (impulse) is introduced. In our case, the impulse is usually a short transient sound such as a starter pistol shot or loud clap that is played in a space to produce a response. Then, the response from that space is recorded. Once recorded, this impulse response is convolved, or combined using a mathematical procedure, with an audio signal to produce a new, reverberant audio signal.

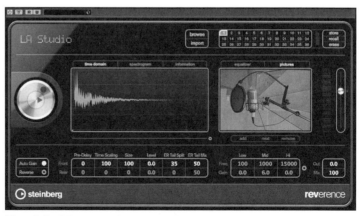

Fig. 4.2: REVerence Convolution Reverb

REVerence is a convolution reverb that comes with Cubase 5 as a VST3 audio plug-in (see Fig. 4.2). It comes with more than 70 impulse responses, many of which are provided by Yamaha, some taken from the company's SREV1 Sampling Reverberator and others recorded in top recording studios and locations around the world. You can also import impulse responses from third-party libraries or from the Internet, so you won't be locked into a certain set of presets.

Getting Around REVerence

REVerence is found in the Inserts tab of an audio track Inspector under the Reverb menu. Once loaded, you'll notice that REVerence is a single-page user interface. While there is a lot of control on this one page, it allows you to dial in a sound very quickly. The interface is divided into vertical thirds, with the top section pertaining to the impulse selection, the middle to graphic displays, and the bottom to parameter settings.

TIP

REVerence works best with a big ASIO buffer size. If you're using it with Cubase 5, your minimum audio buffer size should be 512 samples, and for heavy use, more than 1,000 samples is best. If you're recording, you typically want to have the buffer size as low as possible to reduce latency, but when you're mixing and using REVerence, you will want to increase the buffer size to give it more headroom. REVerence is really designed for mixing, when latency is not an issue. If you need reverb for tracking or overdubbing, Cubase has other built-in tools that are easier on the CPU and work well with small buffer sizes and lower latencies. The RoomWorks SE, for example, is more than adequate for these applications.

In addition to the usual way of browsing presets in the search field at the top, REVerence also has a Browse and Import button in the top section where you can browse programs (which are saved impulses with their associated parameter settings) and import your own. To the right of this are 36 program slots for quick recall. This enables you to load several different programs and audition them on a particular track. When you switch from one program to another, a fade is performed internally from one to the other to avoid an abrupt change, which can cause popping or noise. The LED indicator to the right of the program slots indicates a transition taking place from one program to another. To load a program into a program slot, highlight the slot and click on Browse to open a search, or simply double-click the program slot number to open the search directly. Rounding out the top section are Store, Recall, and Erase buttons.

POWER TIP
Using the REVerence Program Slots for Post-Production

The ability to load many impulse responses into the program slots (and into RAM) and smoothly change from one to another has many practical uses. One use for post-production work would be to place dialog and sound effects in continuously changing environments.

For example, let's say an actor walks from the inside of a church into a small room, and then back into the church. You'll want a large, long reverb on the dialog for the church setting, and as he walks into the small room, you should change this to a shorter, early-reflection room with a wood quality. Then revert the reverb back to the church.

1. Open an instance of REVerence on your dialog and sound effects track(s).

2. Load a large hall (church) impulse response and assign it to a program slot.

3. Load a small, wood room impulse response and assign it to another program slot.

4. As your tracks play back in time with the picture, switch from the large to the small reverb as the actor enters the small room.

5. Change the reverb back to the large reverb when he re-enters the church.

6. After some rehearsal, automate the change and save it with the project.

TIP

Impulse responses can have quite large file sizes, and when you load many into the program slots, they are loaded into RAM in order to transition smoothly from one to the next. If you plan on loading up a lot of impulses at one time, you'll want to make sure you've got plenty of RAM available in your system.

The middle section of the interface consists of a Play button inside a scroll wheel, and two large displays. The Play button introduces a click so you can easily hear the effect with a transient sound. This is really handy, especially for comparing different programs. The scroll wheel adjusts the reverb time or tail length, which can also be done in the control section at the bottom. To the right of this is a large display that has three tabs to display different information. The default Time Domain tab shows the waveform of the impulse response (as seen in Fig. 4.2). The Spectrogram tab shows the impulse response's frequency from bottom to top, with volume represented by color (see Fig. 4.3). The Information tab shows other miscellaneous data about the impulse response (see Fig. 4.4). Under this display is a trim slider that allows you to trim the impulse response from either the beginning or the end. Clicking the button to the right of it activates this slider.

Fig. 4.3: REVerence Spectrogram tab

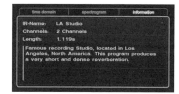

Fig. 4.4: REVerence Information tab

TIP

Trimming the impulse response can be useful in a number of ways. For example, if you want to use a reverb to "fatten" up a snare sound, you can trim it from the end so that the length of the reverb blends into the sound of the snare itself with no tail. Or, trim part of the reverb tail so that it ends abruptly for a "gated" effect.

The display on the far right of the middle section contains two tabs: Equalizer and Pictures. Highlight the Equalizer tab and you can make changes to the EQ of the impulse response by clicking and dragging the low-, mid-, and high-frequency points indicated by the numbers 1, 2, and 3 (see Fig. 4.5). Note that the EQ function must be activated in the control section below for this to work. The default Pictures tab is just that, pictures relating to the impulse response (as seen in Fig. 4.2). In the case of the built-in impulse responses, the pictures give some indication as to the type of space that was recorded. Rounding out the middle section of the interface is an LED meter and a master fader.

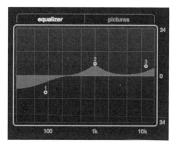

Fig. 4.5: REVerence EQ tab

TIP

When you import your own impulse responses, you can also load a corresponding picture to be displayed. Do this by clicking the Add button under the picture display and navigate to the .jpeg, .gif, or .png file you want to load. You can load up to five files. Use the Next button to scroll through what you have imported and click Remove to delete the ones you don't want to keep.

Parameter Settings

The bottom third of the interface is where you make changes to the impulse response with various parameter settings (see Fig. 4.6). On the far left are settings for Auto Gain (normalization) and Reverse. The next section includes parameter settings for pre-delay, when the reverb starts; time-scaling or reverb time; size of the room; level or reverb volume; ER tail split and ER tail mix, which allow you to split the early-reflection part of the reverb from the tail and decide the mix between the two. The next section controls the EQ. The Low, Mid, and Hi columns correspond to the EQ graph described above and pictured in Fig. 4.5. Here, you can also adjust the frequency and gain as well as activate the EQ in its entirety or each band individually. To the far right of the control section are global controls for output gain and wet/dry mix.

Fig. 4.6: REVerence parameter settings

The trap may be that instead of finding the perfect impulse response, you may be tempted to start with a big hall and adjust the parameters to fit your taste. You can do this, but it's not ideal. It's probably okay if you get somewhat close with your impulse response choice and only have to tweak a little, but drastic changes will most likely degrade the overall sound. This is like most anything; if you change the pitch or time of audio too much, it will not sound natural; if you over-EQ or compress audio, it tends to sound worse than getting a good sound flat and just subtly tweaking it. The same principle applies to radically altering impulse responses.

Surround Impulse Responses

REVerence handles multichannel impulse responses for working in surround. These programs are indicated with an (SR) after the name. When working with these programs, the control section includes Front and Rear rows for parameter settings. You can adjust the level and the ER Tail Mix to create an offset for the rear channels.

POWER TIP
Save Multiple REVerence Programs as a VST Preset

As with all VST3 plug-ins, you can save REVerence programs as a VST preset, which will store the impulse response as well as any parameter settings. Because REVerence can hold up to 36 programs, you have the ability to load several programs into RAM for faster switching, as well as the ability to open this set of programs in another project.

1. Activate a program slot by clicking on it (it will blink).

2. Click Browse or click again to load an impulse response, or use the import function to load one of your own.

3. Make any parameter changes and write any automation changes (as you normally would with the R/W automation buttons).

4. Click the Store button to save your changes to the program slot.

5. Recall a saved program by clicking its program slot (note the crossfade time as described earlier in this chapter).

6. Save as a VST preset by clicking in the Browse field at the top of REVerence and select Save Preset.

INSIDER
Steinberg Software Developer Andreas Mazurkiewicz on What Makes a Quality Convolution Reverb

"The quality of a convolution reverb is in the quality of the rooms themselves, how they are recorded, and the quality of that recording. The math is the math as long as you don't take shortcuts with the mathematical procedure to save some CPU power. For example, you could downsample the reverb tail because you don't need high frequencies. In this case, an impulse response of a room containing high frequencies would have its reverb tail attenuated and not sound as good. So, if you use the correct mathematical procedure, then there is no quality issue.

I started working on this convolution kernel for the Cubase 4 plug-in set, but I needed much more time to do it right. I didn't want a bad convolution reverb with bad workflow, too many or not enough parameters. It had to be right, and by waiting until Cubase 5, I think it's right.

People can import their own impulse responses, and my mathematical procedure is correct, so we thought of other ways to make it a good plug-in. We decided to put all the parameters that are important on one page. Changing parameters is kind of a contradiction because people are recording the actual room, but still want to change it. They say it's a perfect room, but still want to tweak it. How you deal with parameter changes affects the quality of a convolution reverb as well. Let's say I want to change the size of the room. If I do a lousy interpolation or reduction of the impulse response, then you can hear it. Anything you use to tweak the impulse response can affect the quality of the sound as well. You're actually 'resampling the room,' so to speak, so this has to be high quality. Otherwise, it would be the weakest link in the chain. Another example is if you use lousy EQ on your impulse response, the result will sound lousy as well.

The biggest challenge in developing REVerence was parameter smoothing. We had the idea to smooth parameter changes. When you're tweaking the impulse response, you don't want big CPU peaks that might freeze your system, and you don't want to hear clicks or pops when you're working in a studio, so we worked on smooth parameter changes. Unfortunately, they take a bit of time, so if you're using a 10-second impulse response, it will take 10 seconds to fade. But this is, of course, a first version, and I am working

RECORDING AND MIXING 57

to shorten the fading time, or the ability to turn fading off. People may not need all the smoothness when they are auditioning. They will want to hear it instantly. Then you could turn smoothing back on for recording or exporting, for example. This is why we developed the program slot matrix. You can have many impulse responses loaded, and change from one to another very smoothly."

SIGNATURE TRACK AND TEMPO TRACK

Steinberg has added two new track types in Cubase 5: the Signature track and the Tempo track. The goal behind these new track types is to bring the editing of tempo and time signature into the Project window. This allows you to get a quick visual on tempo and time signature as well as better access to their editing capabilities. Now, you can edit time signature and tempo data directly in the Project window, or open a dedicated editor for fine-tuning. Working in this way is familiar and fast; it's the same way you would work with audio and most other types of tracks. This is a good example of how Steinberg keeps moving toward a consistent workflow within Cubase. By creating similar workflows for many tasks, the learning curve is shorter and you can get things done faster and easier than before.

Adding a Signature track and a Tempo track is the same as any other track: simply right-/Control-click in the track list and select the track type from the Add Track menu or add a new track from Cubase's Project menu.

Signature Track

A Signature track shows bars in the timeline, and will have the time signature of the project inserted in a flag at zero (see Fig. 4.7). This initial time signature can be changed by double-clicking in the flag, on the transport bar, or in the track Inspector. Where the timeline shows the time signature in linear bars, the Inspector shows any time signature changes and their corresponding bar number(s) in a list.

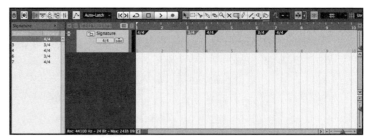

Fig. 4.7: Signature track in the Project window

The track list for a Signature track shows a lock/unlock icon, the time signature at the current locator position, and an icon to open the Process Bars dialog, which we'll get to in a moment.

You can edit your project's time signature from within the Signature track in the Project window by selecting the Pencil tool and clicking in a new flag at the desired bar and typing in the new time signature. This will update the list in the Inspector as well. You can drag this flag to different bars if needed or delete it altogether. This simple process lets you work through your project and manage any time signature changes quickly and easily.

There may be times when you want to work with large sections of a project, and find the timeline approach too tedious. You may need to insert or delete a number of bars, or even change the time signature of a large section in the middle of a project. This is where the Process Bars dialog comes in (see Fig. 4.8). Open this by clicking the Process Bars icon in the track list.

Fig. 4.8: The Signature track Process Bars dialog window

The Process Bars dialog gives you the ability to work with defined sections of a project. To define the sections of the project you want to work with, use the fields under Bar Range. Here, you have a black bar that represents the entire project and a green bar that represents the defined area you want to work with. You can either type in the start bar number and the length (number of bars) you want to work with, or just click the left and right sides of the green bar and drag to highlight the desired section of your project.

Once you have defined a section of the project, go to the Action section of the dialog and select the action you want to perform: Insert Bars, Delete Bars, Reinterpret Bars, or Replace Bars. Finally, select a time signature and click Process. The defined

action will be edited in the project and the results will show up
in the Signature track.

TIP

Use the Reinterpret Bars action to change the time signature without
changing the notes. For example, if you are working with notation in
Cubase and you have a section notated in 3/4 time, but would like to
change it to 6/8 time, the Reinterpret Bars function will change the notation
to fit the time signature without affecting the playback of the notes.

Tempo Track

The Tempo track looks and feels the same as the Signature track,
with some obvious and subtle differences. One of the subtle
differences is that the Tempo track has to be activated in order to
affect the project. A project can either follow a fixed tempo or the
Tempo track. This is determined in the transport bar. Clicking
the Tempo button toggles Cubase between a fixed tempo and
following the Tempo track (see Fig. 4.9).

Fig. 4.9: Tempo track in the transport
bar—Fixed vs. Track

TIP

If the Tempo track is not responding and you're getting frustrated, make
sure the Tempo track is activated in the transport bar!

Like the Signature track, the Tempo track's Inspector contains a
list of edits, and changes are made by clicking in the timeline on
a specified bar and dragging the line up or down to adjust the
tempo (see Fig. 4.10). Tempo change points can be dragged to

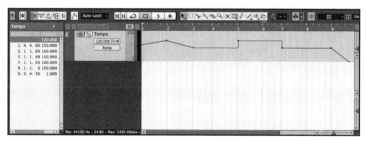

Fig. 4.10: The Tempo track in the Project window

move them or be deleted altogether. Tempo change points are inserted according to the snap value if the Snap function is active in the toolbar.

The track list for the Tempo track also contains a lock/unlock icon, the tempo at the current locator position, and a Process icon, but adds a few new tools. Instead of a Process Bars dialog, there is a Process Tempo dialog, which we'll get to in a moment. There is a Mode button, where you will determine if the tempo you insert "jumps" to the next change or "ramps up" to the next change. Jump is a sudden change to a new tempo, while ramp will gradually increase or decrease the tempo over the length of the time specified by the ramp or curve. You can also select "Automatic" to use the type of insert previously used at that position. Lastly, the track list contains a display range to the right where you can define a range of tempos displayed in the timeline.

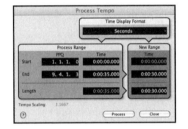

Fig. 4.11: The Tempo track's Process Tempo dialog window

Just as the Process Bars dialog lets you work with large sections of the project's time signature, the Process Tempo dialog lets you work with large sections of a project's tempo (see Fig. 4.11). This time, however, the idea is to define a range of the project and adjust the tempo to fit a specified length or time. The Process Tempo dialog is opened with its icon in the track list. Once open, you can define the time display format in Seconds, Bars+Beats, Timecode, or Samples. You then define the Process Range either by typing it into the dialog fields or setting the right/left locators in the Project window, and then set the New Range. Clicking Process will adjust the tempo to fit the defined range into the new range, and will be reflected in the Tempo track.

POWER TIP
Use the Process Tempo Dialog to Scale a TV Spot

Writing music for TV commercials has at least one common element: the music must adhere to a specifically defined length of time, usually 15, 30, or 60 seconds. Let's say you have a piece of music written in Cubase using VST instruments, and some sliced audio loops that would be perfect for your 30-second TV spot, but it's 35 seconds long. You can use the Process Tempo dialog to adjust the tempo to fit exactly 30 seconds.

1. Set the right/left locators around the desired section in Cubase (in this example it's the entire 35-second project).

2. Add a Tempo track and click the Process Tempo icon to open the dialog.

3. Set the Time Display format to Seconds.

4. Set the Process Range (it should already appear from the setting of the right and left locators—the time should read 0:00:00.000 to 0:00:35.000).

5. Set the New Range with an end point of 0:00:30.000.

6. Click Process.

The Tempo track will now reflect a new tempo to make the project end at exactly 30 seconds to fit your TV spot. Although the music will be played a bit faster, it will probably not change the feel too much, as it's only a five-second change over 30 seconds. If the original music were in 4/4 time at 120 bpm, the new tempo would be 140 bpm. As with any time stretching or crunching, the bigger the tempo change, the more the feel will change.

The Tempo Track Editor

If you prefer to work in an editor in order to keep your Project window focused on audio, MIDI, and VST instruments, the Tempo Track Editor allows you to perform all of the time signature and tempo editing described above, plus a few extras.

The great thing about a dedicated editor is that you have only the tools available that pertain to the type of editing you're performing. This allows you to really focus on the task at hand and work very quickly. Time signature and tempo mapping are often done in the beginning of a project, in which case it would be convenient to hide the tracks from view and use the Tempo Track Editor when you need to make a change.

Open the Tempo Track Editor by selecting it from Cubase's Project menu, or press Command + T. Once open, it will look familiar, as it follows the standard Cubase editor layout (see Fig. 4.12). On the far left there is a column with the tempo range—the same range specified in the track list of a Tempo track. Across the top is a toolbar. Under this are the info line, ruler, the time signature lane, and the tempo map area.

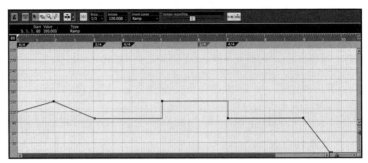

Fig. 4.12: The Tempo Track Editor

The toolbar pulls together the tools from the Project window toolbar that are specific to this editor. The icons from left to right are Activate Tempo Track, Show Info, Tools (pointer, eraser, magnifier, pencil), Autoscroll, and Snap. Next to these are the Snap Value, Tempo, and Insert Curve fields, and a horizontal fader or slider for recording tempo changes in real time. This is like automating tempo changes and is done by simply moving the fader in real time as the project plays back. You will see your tempo changes written into the tempo map as you go. This is handy for making smooth, natural tempo changes, just as you would make fader moves with audio tracks. The last two icons on the toolbar open the Process Tempo dialog and the Process Bars dialog, described earlier.

Under the info line and the ruler, which function the same as in other places in Cubase, you'll find the time signature lane. This functions the same way as in the Signature track. You simply pencil in any desired changes in tempo at a specific bar. Below this is the tempo map area. Again, this functions the same way as a Tempo track and will behave according to the insert curve type and snap values you have set in the toolbar.

Tempo Types

There are some variables that you need to think about when working with tempo and time in Cubase. Some content is flexible or "musical," as Steinberg calls it, and some content is fixed (see Fig. 4.13). MIDI files, REX files, and sliced audio are examples of musical content. The tempo can be changed, and these types of files will respond accordingly. Linear audio files and loops are examples of fixed content, and will not respond to tempo changes. In order to get your fixed content to match the tempo of your project, you can either edit the audio to follow the tempo or make the tempo match the audio.

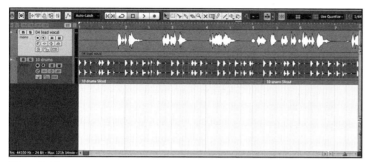

Fig. 4.13: A fixed audio file (above) and a sliced audio file (below) in the Project window

Getting your fixed audio to follow tempo changes is the harder of the two processes, but ultimately is more flexible. You'll need to use an audio file that is rhythmic, so that a beat can be extracted and a tempo calculated. To do this, you'll use the Hitpoints function in the Cubase Sample Editor.

POWER TIP
Using Hitpoints to Slice Audio

1. Open an audio loop in the Sample Editor.

2. Open the Hitpoints tab in the Inspector.

3. Select the Hitpoint mode—all hitpoints, hitpoints with a specific note value, or hitpoints close to a note value (metric bias).

4. Use the sensitivity slider to adjust the hitpoints—you'll want to use a high sensitivity for a better ability to adjust tempo later.

5. Click Slice & Close on the Hitpoint tab.

You now have a sliced audio loop that can be viewed and edited in the Audio Part Editor. Each slice is now an individual event and can now follow tempo changes.

If you are happy with the tempo of your fixed content and want to adapt the project tempo to it, you can use the Time Warp tool. This is useful when you want to build a project around an audio loop or recording with an unknown tempo.

POWER TIP
Use the Time Warp Tool to Match Tempo
to a Fixed Audio File

1. Activate the Tempo track.

2. Select the Time Warp tool from the toolbar in the Sample Editor.

3. Click and drag the start of a bar to the beginning of the audio file or a specific beat within it (the downbeat, for example).

4. This creates a tempo point in the Tempo track, and in the brown timeline in the Sample Editor.

5. You can add more tempo points or edit them in the Tempo track or in the Time Warp tool in the Sample Editor.

Now that you have created a tempo map around the fixed audio file, you can record or add other files to follow it and be in time with the fixed audio file.

AUTOMATION

Automation is the ability to record parameter changes in real time and have Cubase play these changes back in time with the project. Almost everything in Cubase, including its plug-ins, can be automated, which is one of the major advantages of recording and especially mixing with a computer DAW, or "mixing in the box." Common tasks that are automated include fader moves, effects settings, EQ settings, and so on. Depending on how you work and the scale of your projects, you may automate very little or just about everything. It's really a matter of personal choice and practicality. Because we now have access to so much within Cubase, automating tasks can get quite intricate. Steinberg has added some new tools in Cubase 5 to help manage this process and make it easier and faster. They call it Dynamic Automation Handling.

By now, you're most likely familiar with the automation read and write commands, the large green R and red W that appear throughout Cubase. In addition to the track list, channel setting, and mixer windows, these are also commonly found within each plug-in window on the top left corner. Enabling the write automation command (the red W) means Cubase will record your movements in real time as the project plays. To hear these changes played back, simply enable the read automation command (the green R) and play the project back. This process creates automation data that is contained in automation lanes that can be accessed within the track or plug-in you're working on (see Fig. 4.14).

Fig. 4.14: Automation lanes for an audio track

While writing and reading automation is a simple process, keeping track of all of your automation can get overwhelming very quickly. Imagine a film score synced to video, with audio tracks containing music, dialog, and sound effects that require track automation, instrument tracks that need MIDI automation, and several plug-ins that may need to have various settings automated. Keeping track of, enabling/disabling, and editing this automation during a final mix would be a daunting task. You would have to access the automation data from the point where it was recorded, which could literally be hundreds of different places in Cubase.

Enter Dynamic Automation Handling, which is centered around the Automation Panel (see Fig. 4.15). This window unifies all automation functionality within Cubase 5 in one place. To access the Automation Panel, select it from the Project menu. Once open, you'll notice that the panel is made up of a number

Fig. 4.15: The Automation Panel

of columns that fall into three categories, which we'll call the Mode section, the Options section, and the Settings section.

Modes

Automation in Cubase 5 can be handled in one of three modes, which are selected in the far left column of the Automation Panel, or the Mode section. There is also a pull-down menu in the toolbar that enables you to quickly set the mode when writing automation to a track. In Touch mode, Cubase will only write automation data while you're touching the parameter control. Once you let go of the control, the parameter will return to its previous setting. In Auto-Latch mode, once you make a parameter change and let go of the control, the setting will remain instead of returning to its previous setting. Cross-Over mode lets you write new automation over existing automation in order to correct or smooth out any changes you may not like.

Underneath the mode settings you'll find a Trim button. Trim allows you to manipulate existing automation data for channel volume and aux send levels in a very useful way. When the project is stopped and you enable Trim, moving a channel fader will adjust the entire automation curve up or down. This is useful if you are happy with your volume automation curve, but want the overall track to be louder or softer. If you activate Trim while the project is playing, moving a channel fader will adjust the existing automation curve in real time.

TIP

Using Trim during playback doesn't replace your existing automation curve. Instead, Cubase uses the existing automation data and your new fader moves to recalculate a new curve. This is very useful for smoothing a curve or making more subtle corrections to the automation without having to "rerecord" it.

At the bottom of the left column are buttons to enable/disable global automation read and write within your Cubase project.

Options

The middle section of the Automation Panel contains three columns, which make up the Options section. Here you have options for suspending the reading and writing of automation as well as options to show, or open, types of automation lanes. The Suspend Read and Suspend Write columns contain buttons for the most commonly automated tasks: Volume, Pan, EQ, Sends, Inserts, and Mutes. These can be suspended individually, while all other automation parameters are grouped under the Others button. You can click an individual parameter to suspend its read/write capability, or click Suspend Read and Suspend Write to suspend all automation parameters.

P O W E R   T I P
Using Suspend Write Automation

The ability to suspend the writing of certain automation parameters globally has many practical uses. Let's say you want to automate the panning of a rhythm guitar track to pan left and right in time with a drum track during a four-bar break. You may want to mute all other tracks so you can concentrate solely on these two tracks. In this case, you'll want to suspend the writing of mute automation, so the tracks you have muted to work on the guitar part will not be automated to stay muted when you perform your pan automate write.

1. Mute all tracks except the rhythm guitar and the drum track.

2. Go to the Project menu and open the Automation Panel.

3. Select Touch mode, as you only want pan automation written for four bars before the rhythm guitar returns to its original pan position.

4. Enable Global Write Automation in the Automation Panel or enable Write Automation on the rhythm guitar track.

5. In the Suspend Write column, select Mute.

6. In the far right column set the return time (the time to return to the previous pan position once you let go of the pan control after the four bars).

7. Play the project and perform your pan automation moves.

In the same way that you may want to suspend the writing of automation data as in the example above, there are times when you may want to suspend the reading of automation data. This is done in the Suspend Read column.

The third column on the Options section is the Show Options column. Clicking a parameter button will simply open all associated automation lanes within their tracks in the Project window. This is useful if you are working across several tracks on a particular automation function and want to see them all at once. Clicking the Show Used button will open only those automation lanes that contain data. When Show Used is enabled, clicking a parameter will open only the lanes of that parameter that contain data. Hide All simply hides all automation lanes.

Settings

The Settings section is the column to the far right, which contains several global settings. Under the Functions button, you can delete some or all of the automation data in the project, for selected tracks, or for the range between the left and right locators.

The Return Time button is where you set the amount of time it takes for a parameter to return to its previous setting after automation is written in Touch mode.

TIP

You'll want to avoid very low return time settings, as a sudden jump in an automation parameter can cause a "popping" or "crackling" noise. This is why the default is set at 33 ms.

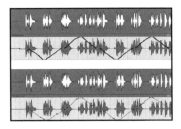

Fig. 4.16: Automation reduction: 0% (top) and 75% (bottom)

The Reduction Level button sets the percentage of reduction in the number of "breakpoints" in an automation curve. When an automation curve is written or performed, a number of breakpoints, or increments, are written into the automation lane for the parameter to follow upon playback. Many of these breakpoints can be removed in order to save CPU overhead without affecting the automation curve (see Fig. 4.16). This is important in large projects where CPU resources are stretched to their limits.

Finally, the Options button contains options for showing audio or MIDI data on automation lanes and continuing automation writing after a transport jump. Showing audio or MIDI data in an automation lane gives you a visual reference for editing and drawing automation data. This is useful if you are zoomed in and have many automation lanes open and the audio or MIDI track is not in view. Continuing to write automation after a transport jump is important if you want to perform multiple passes in cycle mode. Normally, when Cubase jumps locations, the writing of automation stops. This allows you to keep writing automation when Cubase jumps from the end of a cycle back to the beginning.

MIDI Automation

MIDI data can also be automated in Cubase in two ways: as continuous controller data when recording a MIDI part, or as automation data recorded in an Automation track. In the past, these two ways of recording MIDI automation were in conflict. For example, if you were recording a MIDI part and used a breath controller to automate volume as you recorded, it would show up as continuous control data in the MIDI part. If you then automated the volume of that MIDI track in the mixer during mixdown, you would have two types of recorded automation on one track that were in conflict. The result is usually a mess of undesired volume changes.

In Cubase 5, you can merge MIDI part controller data and track automation data in a rule-based system, so the MIDI track knows

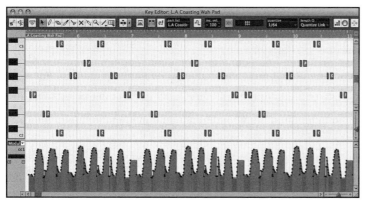

Fig. 4.17: MIDI part with continuous controller data and automation

how to handle the different types of automation. In addition, you can view and edit the continuous control data and automation lane together in one place, which helps you decide how you want the data to be handled (see Fig. 4.17).

Global Setup

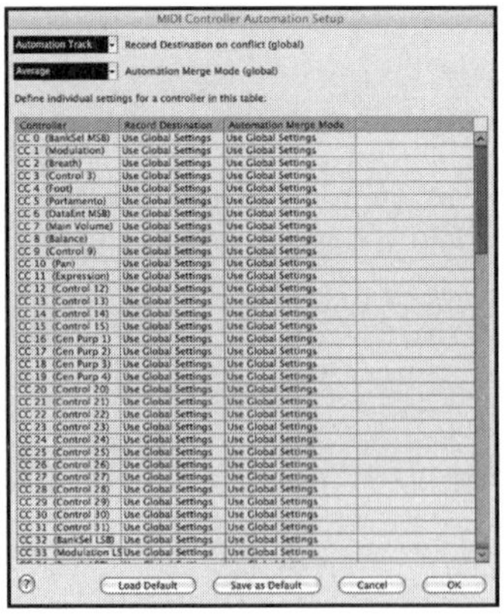

Fig. 4.18: MIDI Controller Automation Setup window

If you have conflicting continuous controller data and track automation data on a MIDI track, you can define how the conflict will be handled in two ways: globally or for individual tracks and controllers. To set the rules globally, use the MIDI Controller Automation Setup window to set the Automation Merge Mode (see Fig. 4.18). This will set the rules for conflicting continuous control and automation data for all MIDI tracks in your project. To access this window, go to the MIDI menu in Cubase and select CC Automation Setup.

In the first pull-down menu, select where Cubase will record new automation data: on a MIDI part or on an Automation track. This will eliminate any conflicts in data being recorded to both places. In the next pull-down menu, select the Automation Merge Mode that will tell Cubase how to play back any conflicting continuous control and automation data that may exist. Selecting Replace 1 – Part Range gives playback priority to the MIDI part, but only when it sees controller data, after which it switches to track automation. Replace 2 – Last Value Continues also gives playback priority to the MIDI part, but instead of switching over to track automation when the part ends, it holds the last continuous controller value. Selecting Average plays back an average of the continuous control and track automation data, and selecting Modulation forces the automation track to modulate, or emphasize, the continuous control automation data for the MIDI part.

Now that the global parameters are set, you can move to the chart below and set up separate record destinations or automation merge modes for individual MIDI controllers, or simply have them use the global settings defined above.

Track Setup

The second way to set up automation merge modes is directly from the Automation track. Right-clicking in the Automation track list will bring up a list of automation merge modes for that specific controller (see Fig. 4.19).

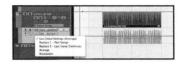

Fig. 4.19: Automation Merge mode MIDI track setup menu

Here, you can select from the same list of automation merge modes that you did in the global setup window, but they will be used only for a specific controller on this specific track. In fact, if there is no conflicting MIDI part controller data and automation track automation, the pop-up menu will not even appear. This takes the guesswork out of knowing when you need to set up automation merge modes.

Workflow

5

As I discussed in the introduction to this book, these days DAW developers seem to be most focused on workflow; how things are done rather how much can be done within a given program. I think this makes sense since modern DAWs contain so many features and have enough power to satisfy most users' needs.

In Cubase 5, Steinberg has continued its refinement of the program's workflow and interface, with several small enhancements, including redesigned MIDI plug-in interfaces for consistency with the updated main interface, the addition of a MIDI monitor to help identify problems with MIDI data, improvements to the user interfaces of the Logical Editor and Input Transformer, and the ability to sort VST plug-ins by vendor.

In this chapter, we'll take a look at some of the main workflow enhancements and features in Cubase 5: VST Expression, VST Sound and MediaBay, and the new Channel Batch Export option. We'll also hear from Steinberg's own Dave Nicholson, who has been an integral part in designing Cubase's workflow and user interface since the early days of Steinberg.

VST EXPRESSION

With the MIDI protocol now more than 20 years old, many people view it as an old, or even obsolete, technology. But MIDI is still heavily relied upon for many tasks in modern DAWs, and is the preferred method of working in some styles of music. This may not be immediately apparent, because MIDI is now more tightly integrated into DAWs and, in many cases, works in the background. Yet in addition to being somewhat of a workhorse for traditional tasks, MIDI continues to be an integral part of new ways of working.

Steinberg has developed new uses for MIDI, such as in Beat Designer, discussed in chapter 2, as well as continued its role in traditional uses. Just about everything in Cubase has some sort of MIDI control, export, or editing option.

VST Expression represents a new MIDI development, with the potential to improve the work of many of those who use VST instruments or sample libraries in their music. The advantage of working with VST instruments and sound libraries is not only the ability to access a large number of sounds, but also the ability to add various articulations, or determine how the sound is performed. This can make your compositions sound more expressive and realistic.

The problem with having several articulations for one sound is that they are difficult to organize and play back inside your DAW. For example, in order to have a violin play a legato note followed by a pizzicato note, different samples need to be triggered. In most cases, this is done with MIDI program changes or key switches. There are other methods that are less common, such as using MIDI channels or even editing MIDI data. Some composers prefer to place each instrument articulation on its own track. These methods work well until you want to transpose or otherwise alter the track. For example, if you have a track that relies on key switches to change articulations and you transpose it, the key switches will be thrown off and the articulation changes will be lost, or worse yet, trigger the wrong articulation. The DAW doesn't know the difference between notes and articulation changes; it views them both as MIDI notes. Placing individual articulation samples on their own tracks can result in very high track counts and can be problematic when editing.

VST Expression negates this problem, and improves creative potential, by creating an Expression Map, which filters out the articulation change data and shows it in a separate controller lane alongside the MIDI notes (see Fig. 5.1). Now, if you alter the MIDI notes, your articulation data is untouched. Conversely, you can edit articulations and keep the same MIDI notes. This is where it becomes apparent that VST Expression doesn't just solve a practical problem, but becomes a way to be creative with articulations. You can even play articulation changes in real time to make your performances more expressive.

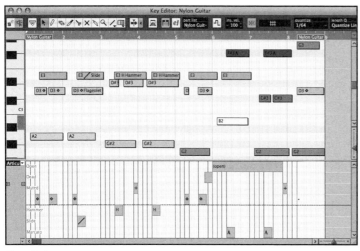

Fig. 5.1: VST Expression

Expression Maps

VST Expression can be accessed from a number of places in Cubase 5, such as the key, score, drum, and in-place editors, where you deal with articulations. There are two ways to access expression maps. One way is via the track presets built into Cubase, which are designated with a "VX" after their file name. When you load an expression map for a MIDI or instrument track, Cubase will read the expressions in the performance and apply the correct articulation from the expression map during playback.

NOTE

Steinberg has included expression maps for use with HALionOne, the program's built-in sample-playback VSTi, and HALion Symphonic Orchestra, a large orchestral library sold separately. You can access expression maps directly from within HALionOne by loading those presets with a "VX" designation at the end of their file names. HALion Symphonic Orchestra VST presets with expression maps begin with "HSO" and end with "VX."

The other way to access VST expression maps is by creating and saving your own. To create a VST expression map, select your MIDI track and open the VST Expression tab in the Inspector. (It is not a default tab, so you'll need to right-/Control-click on the track name at the top of the Inspector and check "VST Expression." Once open, click in the search field and select VST Expression Setup to open the setup window. In this window you will see four sections: Expression Maps, Sound Slots, Output Mapping, and Articulations (see Fig. 5.2).

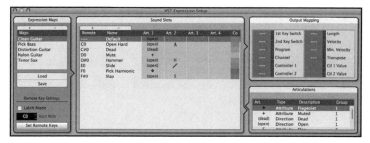

Fig. 5.2: VST Expression Setup window

The first thing you will do is name your expression map by clicking the + sign in the Expression Maps section and entering a name. Next, move to the Sound Slots section, where a sound slot has been automatically added (see Fig. 5.3). Click in the Art.1 column and select or add a custom articulation. This will also automatically name the sound slot, but you can change it if you want to. The Remote column to the left lets you map a slot to an external MIDI device for real-time articulation switching.

Remote	Name	Art. 1	Art. 2	Art. 3	Art. 4	Co
---	Default	(open)				
C0	Open Hard	(open)	Λ			
C#0	Dead	(dead)				
D0	Mute	+				
D#0	Hammer	(open)	H			
E0	Slide	(open)	/			
F0	Pick Harmonic	◊				
F#0	Slap	(open)	S			

Fig. 5.3: VST Expression Setup window: Sound Slots

Next, move to the Output Mapping section to map your articulations to the instrument sounds assigned to the MIDI track for playback (see Fig. 5.4). Here you will find a list of methods used to trigger different articulations (samples) in the instrument you are using on the track (key switch, program change, MIDI channel, or MIDI data; length, velocity, minimum velocity, and transpose). This may seem like a tedious process to set up, but you'll usually use only one method, and fill in one field, for a handful of articulations for a given sound. Also, once you set it up, you can save it for later recall.

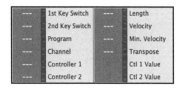

---	1st Key Switch	---	Length
---	2nd Key Switch	---	Velocity
---	Program	---	Min. Velocity
---	Channel	---	Transpose
---	Controller 1		Ctl 1 Value
---	Controller 2		Ctl 2 Value

Fig. 5.4: VST Expression Setup window: Output Mapping

Below the Output Mapping section is the Articulations section (see Fig. 5.5). The articulations you entered in the Sound Slot section appear here and can be edited and assigned to groups. In the Art. column, you can enter a symbol or text to appear in the editors. The Type column specifies whether you want the articulation to be applied to a single note (Attribute) or to all notes following the articulation and until another articulation is used (Direction). Next, you can enter a description and assign the articulation to a group.

Art.	Type	Description	Group
◊	Attribute	Flageolet	1
+	Attribute	Muted	1
(dead)	Direction	Dead	1
(open)	Direction	Open	1
S	Attribute	Slap	2
H	Attribute	Hammer	2
/	Attribute	Slide	2
Λ	Attribute	Marcato	2

Fig. 5.5: VST Expression Setup window: Articulations

Grouping articulations allows you to set exclusions and priorities so that playback will sound more natural. You can assign articulations in up to four groups. Articulations within the same group can never be played together, whereas articulations in different groups can. For example, a violin cannot play arco (bowed) and pizzicato (plucked) at the same time, so these articulations should be placed in the same group. It is possible, and likely, to want a violin to play arco, staccato, and with an accent all at the same time, which would require three articulations. These should be placed in different groups.

Furthermore, groups determine the priority of playback, with group 1 being the highest and 4 being the lowest. In the example above, let's say arco is assigned to group 1, staccato to group 2, and accent to group 3. VST Expression will now search for a sample to play back that matches all three of these articulations, beginning with group 1, then 2, then 3. This is important, because if a sample matching all three articulations cannot be found, it will begin by playing an arco violin sample, which is the most likely to be found, and also the most difficult to simulate with editing. If an arco sample is found that is not staccato or accented, you can edit the sample to simulate these articulations: simply shorten the length of the MIDI note to make it staccato and increase the velocity to give it an accent.

The last step in setting up your own VST expression map is Remote Key Settings. Here, you can set up which external MIDI keys will trigger your articulations. This is useful if you prefer to "play" your music into Cubase rather than add articulations in the editors. To do this, click the Set Remote Keys button and enter the start key, or the first MIDI note to trigger your first sound slot (see Fig. 5.6). Then select Key Mapping, or which notes you want to use to trigger the sound slots, and click OK. Now you will be able to trigger your articulation changes from a MIDI keyboard.

Fig. 5.6: VST Expression Setup window: Set Remote Keys dialog box

Now that your expression map is set up, save it by clicking Save in the Expression Map section. You can recall this expression map later by opening the Setup dialog again and clicking Load in the Expression Map section.

VST Expression in the Editors

Now that you know how to access and create expression maps, let's look at how they are applied in Cubase. As I said earlier, VST Expression is available in several places in Cubase. First, you can pull up the VST Expression tab in a track's Inspector, and it will show the sound slots and articulations for the expression map that is used (see Fig. 5.7). As the notes are played, green arrows light up the articulation that is applied. This is a good way to monitor what is going on, but you cannot make any changes here. Most of the time, you'll probably work with articulations in the Key and Score Editors.

IN THE KEY EDITOR

Double-click on the MIDI part in the Project window to open the Key Editor. As you would expect, the first thing you'll see is the MIDI notes in the timeline. Each note not only contains the note name, but also any associated articulation symbol and name (you'll need to be zoomed in far enough to see all three). Under the MIDI notes are the MIDI controller lanes as usual. However, in the pull-down menu to the left of the MIDI controller lanes, you'll find an option for articulations. Selecting this opens the Articulations controller lane and displays the VST expression map associated with the current sound (as seen earlier in Fig. 5.1).

The Articulations controller lane is where you'll apply (if not through MIDI triggering) and edit your articulations (see Fig. 5.8). The vertical green lines correspond to each MIDI note in the timeline. If you have played articulations into the track via MIDI, you will see colored blocks appear in the controller lane under the note with its associated symbol, which correspond to the written articulations (sound slots) on the left-hand side of the lane. You can add articulations with the pencil tool or via Alt/Option, as well as delete, move, or otherwise edit them, just as you would with MIDI data. You can have multiple controller lanes open at a time, which means you can edit MIDI notes, articulations, velocity, pitch bend, or any other MIDI data in separate lanes, together in one window. It's an extremely fast way of working.

NOTE

Attributes and Directions will appear and act differently in the Articulations controller lane. If you enter an Attribute, it will appear for just the duration of the note it's applied to, and will only affect that note. A Direction will appear as a solid block and will affect all notes until another articulation is entered for that note or in the same group.

You can add articulations by highlighting a MIDI note and accessing the Articulations pull-down menu in the info line, but I find that using the controller lane is much faster. This can be useful if you don't want to have the Articulations controller lane open for some reason.

Fig. 5.7: VST Expression in the Inspector

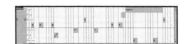

Fig. 5.8: Articulations in the Key Editor

IN THE SCORE EDITOR

For those of you who work with notation, the Score Editor is a logical place to work with articulations. Select a track and open the Score Editor. You'll now see your track in notation form with any associated articulations written directly into the score (see Fig. 5.9). To add articulations from your VST expression map, first click on the Show Symbols icon to open the Symbols Inspector. Then click VST Expression and select the articulation you want to insert. Now, when you mouse back over to where you want to insert the articulation, the pencil tool appears. Simply draw it into place. You can also delete, change, and move articulations in the Score Editor.

Fig. 5.9: VST Expression in the Score Editor

TIP

You can set a different color for different articulations in order to easily distinguish them from other symbols and notes in the score. To do this, go to Cubase > Preferences > Scores > Colors for Additional Meanings, and click on the color palette next to VST Expression.

INSIDER
Steinberg Senior Product Planning Manager
Arnd Kaiser on VST Expression

"VST Expression is the beginning of something new. When you look at VST instruments, how far can we go to really emulate acoustic instruments? Using multiple articulations that can be switched and using some real-time controls is one thing, but there are certain limits; limits on the instrument side with sampling technology and limits on the MIDI side. MIDI is really just hitting a certain note at a certain time with a certain velocity, and that's pretty much it. So we see a lot of potential on both the instrument side and also on the host, or Cubase, side. We can build on this new VST Expression technology and expand it to make it even more powerful, to the point where Cubase can become a real expressive conducting tool by itself. Not just recording, playback, and editing, but really being able to realize more expressive performances."

VST SOUND AND MEDIABAY

One of the major advancements in Cubase 4 was the introduction of SoundFrame and MediaBay, which together were a big step in solving a growing media management problem that many Cubase users faced. With the proliferation of media types from both internal and external sources, finding, auditioning, and keeping track of audio, video, MIDI, and other types of files had become more and more difficult. Steinberg's answer to this problem was a system of organizing various media types (SoundFrame) into a database (MediaBay) to help users find, audition, and track their files.

While the concept was praised, it could only be applied to Steinberg content that adhered to the company's new VST3 plug-in protocol, which meant little to no third-party content could be managed with the system. You could manually add and set up your own content to be used with the system, but it was a very tedious process and took a lot of time for large libraries, VST instruments, and other types of files.

MediaBay was also held back by the late release of the VST3 SDK (Software Developers Kit), which allowed third-party companies to update their plug-ins and develop new plug-ins to work in the MediaBay database. Once released, it took these companies some time to catch up, and as a result MediaBay was slow to be adopted by Cubase users, and is still something many have not explored.

With Cubase 5, Steinberg has expanded the SoundFrame concept and now calls it "VST Sound." The change in name indicates that it's an open system to encourage third-party development. VST Sound brings audio files, video files, MIDI files, REX files, VST sound loops, VST3 presets, track presets, VST instruments, pattern banks, and even project files together under the MediaBay database.

The release of Cubase 5 was important, as MediaBay has been improved, and many third-party companies are now developing heavily for VST3, allowing more content to take advantage of the system.

MediaBay

MediaBay is a powerful search engine within Cubase 5 that allows you to browse, search, and organize your content into a number of categories and with a number of attributes, regardless of their location. You can access MediaBay by opening the Cubase Media menu and selecting Open Media Bay (or use the default key command F5).

MediaBay is opened in default view with all of its sections open: the Browser section on the left, the Viewer section in the middle, the Tag Editor on the right, and the Scope section under the Viewer (see Fig. 5.10). Any of these sections can be hidden by clicking them off in the info line at the bottom of the screen.

Fig. 5.10: MediaBay

THE BROWSER

The Browser on the left-hand side of MediaBay works the same way as your computer browser window, except that it adds the ability to scan your system for specific types of media content. A few parameters in this section allow you to browse and organize your content. Activate the Deep Results icon if you want to see results for subfolders, the Rescan on Select icon if you want MediaBay to perform a fresh scan every time you select a folder, and the Add Folder icon to customize how your content is organized. When you select a folder in the Browser section, its contents will appear to the right in the Viewer section. You can have MediaBay scan and display all the content on your system, or browse specific locations if you know what you're looking for.

You can narrow the focus of what you are browsing by using the Full and Focus tabs. The Full tab will show your entire system, whereas the Focus tab will only show the selected folder and subfolders. Additionally, you can choose to exclude all content that is not being managed by MediaBay by clicking the circle icon above the browser window.

POWER TIP
Use Browser Presets for Frequently Accessed Content

Often you will find yourself coming back to the same location to look for content. You may be working over long periods of time on a project that requires specific content, or you may simply have your favorites that you come back to time and again. Rather than spending the time browsing and navigating to a specific folder, you can create a browser preset to go directly to it.

1. Select the folder you frequently visit in the Browser section.

2. Click the Add Browse Location Preset icon (the + icon).

3. Name the preset and click OK.

4. Access your preset with the Select Browse Location Preset pull-down menu (the small down arrow to the right of the + and − icons).

THE VIEWER

The Viewer, the middle section shown in Fig. 5.10, is where MediaBay displays your individual content files as well as their associated categories, attributes, and other details. New to Cubase 5 is the ability to filter file types to further focus your content searches.

The bar along the top of this section includes a Category tab, a new Details tab, and a File Type filter. The File Type filter is a series of icons that represent the file types to be included in the displayed results (see Fig. 5.11). You can choose to display audio and MIDI files, MIDI loops, pattern banks, track and VST presets, video files, and project files.

Fig. 5.11: MediaBay filter icons

Once you decide which file types you want displayed, you can narrow your search further using the Category tab and the Details tab below. The Category tab contains columns for category, sub-category, style, sub-style, character, and key, allowing you to quickly find the file category that fits your needs. You can then click to the Details tab and further filter your results by selecting any number of the attributes that you want your file to contain (see Fig. 5.12).

Fig. 5.12: The MediaBay Details tab, new in Cubase 5

POWER TIP
Using MediaBay to Find a Specific File on Your System

New to Cubase 5, the Details search tab lets you find a specific file on your system by name or other file attribute. This is handy if you know what file you want to use, but are not sure where it is stored.

1. Select the root folder of your hard drive in the Browser section (this will ensure that MediaBay searches the entire system).

2. Open the Details tab in the Viewer section.

3. In the field to the right of "Any Attribute" and "contains," click and enter all or part of the file name you're looking for.

4. As you type, MediaBay will search for files that contain your input and display the results.

5. Select the desired file from the results display.

This is a simple name search, but the new Details search tab lets you perform similar searches using many attributes in the pull-down menu.

Experiment with searches using different attributes, and you'll get the hang of it quickly.

Filtering your results using the File Type filter, Category tab, and Details tab gives you access to a lot of information about a given file. In many cases, using all of these together will narrow your results too much and not give you very many options. You can use these tools together or separately and in any order to get your desired results. Experiment to come up with a procedure that's comfortable and productive for you.

Another useful way of searching for files is to use the context-sensitive menu. This is especially useful for finding files with similar attributes that you may want to use along with a file you've already selected.

POWER TIP

Finding Similar Files with a Context-Sensitive Menu Search

1. Highlight a file in the display results and right-/Control-click on it.

2. Scroll to "Search for…" and a pop-up menu appears with a list of all of the attributes for the selected file.

3. Select a common attribute that you want to look for.

4. The results will now display all found files with the selected common attribute.

THE TAG EDITOR

On the right side of the MediaBay is the Tag Editor (as shown in Fig. 5.10). This displays all of the attributes associated with a media file, and gives you the ability to edit and create your own tags for custom searches and organizing your content.

There are two tabs in this section, the Managed tab and All tab. The Managed tab shows all tags that are available for manipulation while the All tab shows these along with those that cannot be changed, such as date created, file size, plug-in vendor, etc.

Fig. 5.13: The Manage Tags window

To manage or manipulate tags, click the Manage Tags icon at the bottom of the screen to open the dialog window (see Fig. 5.13). This dialog contains the tags, columns, filters, and so on that you can manipulate. Here, you have the ability to add or remove tags, reclassify files, and decide where tags will be displayed in MediaBay. You also have the ability to add your own custom tags to files.

POWER TIP

Adding Custom Tags to Your Content

You may find it convenient to add additional tags to existing content, or create tags for your original content. Let's say you're a sound designer, and you've recorded your own custom samples. These samples will have attributes such as date, file size, length, and so on, but will not have any meaningful attributes for categorization in MediaBay. You can create tags for these using the following procedure.

1. Select the desired file in the Viewer section.

2. Open the Manage Tags dialog by clicking the icon at the bottom of the screen.

3. Click the Add User Tag (+) icon.

4. Name the tag and define its type.

5. Enter a type value (if it's a number).

6. Click OK.

The newly created tag will show up in red at the bottom of the list in the Manage Tags dialog window. From here, it can be managed and searched like any other tag.

THE SCOPE

The final part of the MediaBay interface is the Scope section at the bottom of the window (see Fig. 5.14). This area allows you to audition files before bringing them into your project. You can preview audio files and loops, MIDI files and loops, VST instrument and track presets, and pattern banks. Each file type will bring up a corresponding set of controls in the Scope section to help you audition it for your project.

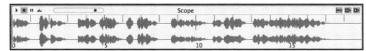

Fig. 5.14: MediaBay Scope section

If you select an audio file, for example, the waveform will be displayed under a small transport and level slider. Simply push Play to audition the file. On the far right of the Scope section are three icons. The first is Auto Play, which automatically and continuously plays the file when selected. This is handy when clicking through many files to find one that sounds right for your project. The next icon is Play in Project Context, and will play the project back with the file so you hear them together. The last icon is Sync to Main Transport, which gives you control of the tempo and other transport controls while auditioning files.

Selecting MIDI files, VST presets, and other file types will bring up controls that aid in auditioning, similar to the way I've described with audio files, but with controls unique to the file type. For example, you will need to select a MIDI file for a VST instrument preset or a VST instrument for a MIDI file.

TIP

Cubase 5 has a new virtual keyboard built into the transport bar. Rather than opening a MIDI file, you can use it to audition VST instrument presets in MediaBay. Open the virtual keyboard by navigating to the Cubase Devices menu and selecting Virtual Keyboard.

Other MediaBay Browsers

Cubase 5 includes two variations of MediaBay that are set up for the most common types of file browsing—loops and sounds, which probably make up the largest number of files on most systems. Steinberg calls these two variations of MediaBay the Loop Browser (see Fig. 5.15) and the Sound Browser (see Fig. 5.16). They are accessed in Cubase's Media menu just under MediaBay. Since these are simply copies of MediaBay with certain settings as the defaults, all of the same techniques applied in MediaBay can be applied to them. If you find yourself working with loops a lot, you may want to go to the Loop Browser first for its default settings. Likewise, if you work with a lot of VST instruments, the Sound Browser may be your first choice.

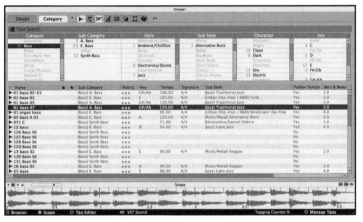

Fig. 5.15: The Loop Browser

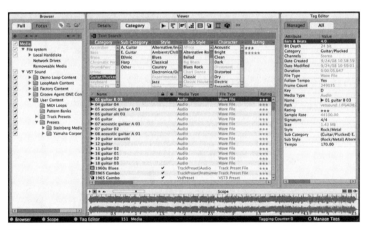

Fig. 5.16: The Sound Browser

CHANNEL BATCH EXPORT

Cubase has long had the ability to mix down audio internally for exporting a final stereo mix (or a 5.1 surround mix since the Cubase SX version). This is one of the biggest advantages of working "in the box": once you've recorded, edited, and mixed your project, you can export a final stereo mix for the mastering house or to burn directly to CD/DVD.

In past versions of Cubase, this mixdown process was limited to stereo or 5.1 mixes. These are still available, of course, and it is a simple process. Cubase mixes down everything you hear that's in the audio domain, including output buses, audio channels, and mixer channels. You'll want to record any MIDI tracks that trigger external instruments as audio within Cubase in order to include them in the mixdown.

To mix down to a stereo file:

1. Place the left and right locators around the audio to be mixed down.

2. Read-enable any automated tracks.

3. Mute or delete any unwanted tracks.

4. Go to File > Export > Audio Mixdown.

5. Make sure Channel Batch Export is unchecked and check Stereo Out.

6. Select your desired export settings in the Export Audio Mixdown dialog box.

7. Click Export.

Cubase 5 has added an important component to the audio mixdown function: Channel Batch Export, which adds the ability to select individual channels for export without mixing them down (see Fig. 5.17). This is important if you want to move your project to a different DAW system for further work or collaboration, or if you want to archive a project without it being tied to a specific platform. Channel Batch Export allows you to export audio channels in a number of different file formats.

Another important feature of Batch Channel Export is that it will create audio files that equal the length between the right and left locators. This makes all files of equal length so they can be easily time-aligned when imported into another DAW. Simply insert the audio files at zero in the timeline.

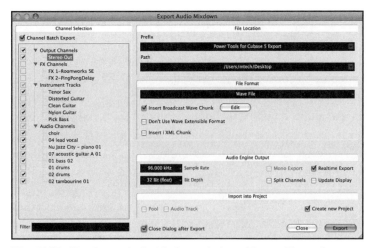

Fig. 5.17: The Export Audio Mixdown window with new Channel Selection section

To use Channel Batch Export:

1. Place the left and right locators around the audio to be mixed.

2. Go to File > Export > Audio Mixdown.

3. Make sure Channel Batch Export is checked.

4. Select the channels you want to export (you can include the stereo mix).

5. Make your desired export settings in the Export Audio Mixdown dialog box.

6. Click Export.

TIP

If your project contains a lot of tracks, it may get tedious searching through the channel display to find the tracks you want to include in the export. Use the Filter field at the bottom to find certain tracks using keywords that correspond to the way you've named your tracks.

Other Export Options

There are two other ways to export or archive individual audio tracks. The first is to export files using OMF, or the Open Media

Framework protocol. This is a file type intended to be platform independent. However, standardization of OMF has been difficult, and there is no guarantee that future platforms will be able to open an OMF archive. It is safer to archive your project as audio files, and preferably in a few different formats.

The second way is to create audio "stems" from your tracks. This process takes audio tracks of different lengths and makes them all the same for export/import or archiving purposes. I learned this process years ago from Steinberg's Greg Ondo, and it may help you understand the process and application of Channel Batch Export.

1. Set the Right/Left Locators around the project.

2. Go to Edit > Select All.

3. Go to Transport > Locate Selection.

4. Right-/Control-click and select the Range Tool.

5. Go to Edit > Select All.

6. Go to Audio > Bounce Selection.

Now all of the audio tracks in your project are the same length. If you export the files and import them into another DAW at zero, they will play back correctly in the timeline. Channel Batch Export works much the same way in the background of Cubase to simplify this process. It also performs the final step of exporting the audio.

INSIDER
Steinberg GUI Architect Dave Nicholson on the Cubase Workflow and Graphical User Interface

How are you involved with Cubase?

I am the user-interface architect. The architect is someone who tries to give direction to the final product. This is important for a program that over 20 years has moved from having a very clear aim for a particular customer base—people with one or two MIDI keyboards and a small computer—to people trying to run complete studios with the software. We have to keep an eye on this monster that does everything and help users find a way through it. I have a very strong view that Cubase shouldn't be seen as a collection of programs. It's not a program suite. It is one program, which is meant to do all these things.

So you look at the user interface, but also the workflow of Cubase.

"Workflow" is a word I've been writing on the wall now for the last few years. It's interesting how different people understand some words differently. When I use it, I'm meaning it in terms of how something fits the way we do things. Is it "Steinberg-like"? Is it consistent with other things we've already done? If it's not, do we have to modify things we've done before to bring them in line with the ideas we have now? Take a piece of Cubase that's been there for a while: the Key Editor, for example. The way you work with events there has not changed a great deal since the program was created. Now, we look at completely new areas of the program and try and reconcile the change between the two.

Workflow for some developers means which buttons to push on a certain part of the screen to do something in the program. I would call this *micro-workflow*. I deal with *macro-workflow*: how the user goes about doing things in Cubase. We need to bring the two together to optimize the program.

How do you reconcile different areas of development in a workflow sense?

It works on many different levels. There is no standardized development process, or better said, no standardized idea process. You can't say that all ideas are worked out on paper and then we go away and program them. It may be that one group of developers or one developer has started an idea and he has something. You have a particular part of the program which someone has worked on—that's their creative energy, and how do you make it fit in with the whole thing?

Ideas for Cubase come in many different ways. Developers are given the remit to develop their ideas. You also have the classic way, where the marketing guys, working with the people in product planning, look at what our competitors are doing and what the weaknesses are in Cubase. What they then come to us with varies from a general idea that we need to add more weight to an area of the program to a complete plan for a specific feature.

How do the actual graphics of the UI come into the process?

There are two sides to it: the user interface architecture and the actual user interface. This process I call the wallpapering. At some point it has to be decorated. Into this comes a whole different area of aesthetics, which a lot of people confuse with the architecture.

The aesthetics are constantly changing. The program looks different now than it did when we were on Cubase SX. That's when I started doing the aesthetics of Cubase. Everyone was doing a little bit, and it got glued together, and that was the way it was developing. I became involved at that point and said, "Let's not just do the bare minimum, let's try and move from a world where software would look like it came fresh from the developers." Now, the presentation of the data is just as important as the data itself.

There are many types of customers: younger, older, this type of musician or that type of musician. There is no one group we are working to make Cubase for. And this is also part of the design aesthetic—we don't try and cater to one particular type of music or musician. In Cubase 5, we very deliberately put more beat tools into it, and they are themselves the younger part of the program. For example, I went to one of our product demos recently, and the people who turned up were not the 16- and 17-year-olds; they were a mature group. And I mean that in a positive sense. They were a wide age range; it wasn't just one kind of person turning up. If we were to hook our wagon to just one group of users and one music style, that's not the way to build a future for Cubase.

With this idea of keeping it wide, in Cubase 5 we specifically said we are going to deal with the people who are using tempo tools, sequenced instruments, and loop manipulation tools. But let's do it the Steinberg way. And the way we've done it is the fact that they are plug-ins. It's your choice as a user to turn this aspect of Cubase on or off. It could be that someone gets their new Cubase 5, opens up the new LoopMash plug-in and says, "That's not for me." I'm okay with that. It would be great if they get inspired by it, but it's not as if we've modified the entire program to accommodate this one way of working or for one style of music.

Is this the idea behind the customization of Cubase from color or entire window sets, which really began with Cubase SX?

Yes. I'll give you two examples: the toolbar across the top of the screen and the Inspector. I started with the toolbar, and the direction it was going in was that everyone has a feature that absolutely has to be in the toolbar. The more things that I put in the toolbar, I started to realize the problem: the color menu disappeared! In those days everything had to fit on a monitor with 800 pixels. Now it all has to fit on 1,280 pixels. So what people were saying is, Well, just make everything smaller. You can do a bit of that, until the point where you've got such a mess of things up there that there is no orientation anymore.

I use a model for how I think people actually find things. People tend to spiral in on things with their eyes. If you are presented with many objects, your eye finds groups, and then in groups locates things. People think it's instant, but it's really a process when you're presented with a lot of items. You circle in and find that one object. So making them smaller and putting more of them in makes this argument that we now have more in there and the program is a better value. I say no. I don't think it's a better value because it's not easy to use.

This meant that the toolbar could be trimmed to the way particular people wanted to use it. But it also brought up another piece of very important information, which is that a number of users never discover that they can customize it. Some things must disappear, and people think that it's gone entirely when it's not. For a lot of people, if you go too far with customization, you've got to be even more careful about the default settings. The defaults become far more important. There are always pressures to put more on the screen, so you have to decide what is included with the end user in mind. What would you expect them to turn on and off? How much of the manual would you expect them to read?

This idea of customizing the toolbar went further, and you now see it in the Inspector. The Inspector from the original version of Cubase 20 years ago was just a flat panel with about eight or nine controls on it. You could turn the whole panel on or off, but in itself it wasn't paged. You opened it for a particular track class and particular part, and there was a list of parameters: things like the name, the transposition, the delay, and velocity. Eventually a few more things came, but there was a particular point where we moved to this Inspector, and it became paged. There were general settings: the inserts, the sends, the channel strip, the surround EQ, and so on.

The Inspector default, when we first did it, included five objects, or five paged items. My theory is that five items is about the maximum you can actually look at without having to count to find one of them. It's the top one, it's the bottom one, it's the middle one, and it's the one above the middle one or the one below the middle one. You don't need to think about it. Put six in there, and you begin to count. Six is difficult because the eye has a harder time finding the middle one. Seven is actually easier for the eye to find the middle one, but harder to find something in the top portion or the bottom portion.

Customization is a very important tool for a program that always gets bigger, but my view is that the more customization you offer, the defaults become far more important.

Do you think the Arrange page, now the Project window, was the biggest innovation in the development of Cubase?

There are so many things where you can say it was the first. But I would say yes, this visualization we called VISP. When you have too many marketing people and the coffee is too hot, they eventually start generating acronyms! Visual Song Processing or VISP. And we were the first to have it.

I have to tell a personal story about this. I was a very, very bad keyboard player, and back then Pro24 was to me an absolute revelation. I could put the music I had in my head into the machine and I could edit it! I could actually go further than my own ability. I had a problem with hitting wrong keys. I know what I wanted to play, but I hit so many keys around the keys I wanted to play. In the List Editor, in those days called the Grid Editor, I could see these events and remove all the places where I clipped the side of another key and then quantize it. That to me was it! I thought, "It doesn't get any better than this." But then I saw Cubase beta version 0.808. I put this diskette in the machine, started it up, and it was like the world that I had in my head was now on the screen. I opened up my Pro24 songs in Cubase and could see it! And to not only see it but also actually be able to move it around was astounding! So I think that was the big innovation, Visual Song Processing, the Arrange page, the Project window, the idea that data was in little blocks and you could just move it around. An absolute godsend!

Hardware Integration

6

Steinberg has traditionally positioned itself as an "open-platform" company, meaning that you can use other brands of hardware with Cubase and other Steinberg software. This has been successful for the most part due to the widespread adoption of the ASIO (Audio Stream In/Out) driver protocol. Steinberg makes developing ASIO drivers easy and accessible for third-party manufacturers, and therefore makes it easy for them to integrate audio hardware with Cubase.

While the benefit of this to users has been the ability to keep and use their favorite hardware when new versions of Cubase are released, third-party manufacturers have, in most cases, written their own mixing applications as a bridge between their hardware and Cubase. In doing this they solve some problems and create others. On the positive side, they add routing flexibility and the ability for the hardware to be used as a stand-alone mixer. The downside is that there is an intermediate software step between the hardware and the DAW. This can create compatibility issues as well as add to the development time for third-party manufacturers when new versions of the software are released.

One of Yamaha's biggest promises when it acquired Steinberg in 2005 was to produce tightly integrated hardware/software solutions using both companies' decades of experience, while maintaining the open flexibility Steinberg has become known for. In 2008, after a couple of years of development, we saw the first Steinberg-branded hardware co-developed with Yamaha: the MR816 Series Advanced Integration DSP Studio and the CC121 Advanced Integration Controller.

"Advanced Integration" sounds like marketing speak, and to some extent it is, but it means that these hardware units work together with Cubase in ways that third-party hardware units can't. Of course, Cubase will still work with your favorite ASIO-based hardware unit, but these new Steinberg/Yamaha units link directly to features within Cubase, with no need for intermediate software. These "hooks" into Cubase are what makes them different from other hardware.

MR816X AND MR816CSX

The single most important piece of hardware in computer audio recording, other than the computer, is the audio interface used to connect your instruments and microphone to your computer and into Cubase. Yamaha has had a long history of making audio interfaces, and a long relationship with Steinberg in getting them to communicate with Cubase. Before acquiring Steinberg, Yamaha used a system called "Studio Connections" to connect its audio hardware with Cubase. As discussed above, this was the intermediate software step between hardware and software. With the release of the MR816 Series, Studio Connections is no longer an external link, as Steinberg's software developers and Yamaha's hardware developers have integrated the hardware directly with the software for the first time. The result is a very clean and efficient system that lets you work very quickly.

At first glance, the MR816 Series interfaces look like most other FireWire audio interfaces (see Fig. 6.1). They have analog inputs and outputs with microphone preamps, digital inputs and outputs, synchronization inputs and outputs, gain controls, digital signal processing (DSP), headphone outputs, and FireWire connectors. Sounds familiar, right? However, the big advantage is how these new interfaces work with Cubase.

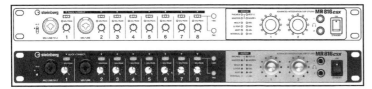

Fig. 6.1: MR816CSX front panel

The MR816X/CSX front panel sports two of the eight mic preamps, each with a gain control, signal/peak indicator, and a multifunction button. Input 1 has a Hi-Z switch for direct connection of a guitar or other high-impedance instrument source. To the right of these are gain controls, signal/peak indicators, and multifunction buttons for inputs 2 through 8. Next are selection buttons for 48V phantom power and a pad (–26 dB), which when pushed engage the multifunction buttons for each channel to turn on and off.

The next section, the first in the silver part of the front panel, contains a series of LED indicator lights that tell you the status of various parameters. The top section tells you what the front panel is controlling at any one time: the headphone volume, the master volume, the REV-X Reverb, or the Morphing Sweet Spot Channel Strip (MR816CSX only). The next set of LEDs tells you where the word clock synchronization source is coming from: the word clock input (WCLK), the S/PDIF input, the ADAT input, or the internal source. If there is no word clock source set, these LEDs will flash. The last set of LEDs indicates the sample rate of the MR816: 44.1, 48, 88, or 96 kHz.

A WORD ABOUT WORD CLOCK

Word clock can often be overcomplicated. Simply put, word clock is a signal produced by a digital device (the master) that allows other digital devices (the slaves) to follow its timing so that the audio signals passed between all devices will be synchronized. If the signals are not synchronized, you may hear noise, or sending audio between devices may not work at all.

ASSIGN lamp	Knob 1	Knob 2
PHONES	Adjusts the volume level output from the headphone jack (∩) 1 on the front panel.	Adjusts the volume level output from the headphone jack (∩) 2 on the front panel.
MASTER	Adjusts the master volume level output from the OUTPUT 1 – 8 jacks on the rear panel.	Adjusts the master volume level output from the S/PDIF OUT jack and OPTICAL OUT jack on the rear panel.
REV-X	Adjusts the reverb time of the internal Reverb effect unit (REV-X).	Adjusts the return level from the internal Reverb effect unit.
MORPH*	Adjusts the DRIVE parameter of the internal compressor.	Morphs the Sweet Spot Data of the internal compressor.

* Only available on the MR816 CSX.

Fig. 6.2: MR816 knob control chart

To the right of the LEDs are two large control knobs, which control the various parameters of the MR816. You select which parameters you want to control by pressing the first knob, and change the values by turning them. As you press the first knob, the status LEDs will tell you what parameters can be adjusted by the knobs (see Fig. 6.2). Rounding out the front panel of the MR816 are two headphone jacks and a power switch.

On the back panel (see Fig. 6.3) you'll find, from left to right, the power connector, S/PDIF and ADAT digital connections, two FireWire connections, word clock in/out, eight TRS balanced output connections, mic preamp inputs 3 – 8 (continued from the front panel), and two insert connections for inserting external audio processors. These two inserts correspond to inputs 1 and 2 on the front panel only.

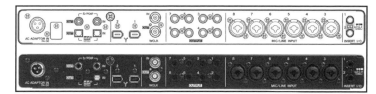

Fig. 6.3: MR816CX back panel

The MR Editor

I mentioned that one of the advantages of having hardware and software developed by the same company is direct integration without the need for intermediate software for communication between the two. While the MR816 and Cubase can talk directly (covered in more detail below), Steinberg includes a software utility called the MR Editor that allows you to set up and save MR816 preset configurations (see Fig. 6.4). This utility looks and works like a mixer, with various connections and controls for routing signal, applying effects, and controlling gain structure. The MR Editor is also handy when you want to use the MR816 in stand-alone mode. The MR816 will remember its last configured state and boot this way. I typically save a standard mixer setup so that I can just flip the MR816 on and start playing the various instruments I have attached to it without first turning on the computer or launching Cubase.

Fig. 6.4: The MR Editor

The MR Editor should be very intuitive for anyone who has used a mixer, so I won't go into detail here about its various controls and parameters. For a complete description, refer to page 33 of the MR816 manual.

Quick Connections

While the MR Editor is primarily intended to allow the MR816 to work as a stand-alone mixer, the big advantage of this hardware is its ability to "hook" into Cubase directly. Once you have the Yamaha Steinberg FW ASIO driver from the "Tools for MR" CD installed, the MR816 not only passes audio directly to the track inputs in Cubase, but also allows you to control input routing as well as reverb and compression settings right from the front panel.

Quick Connect is a feature that allows you to quickly change your input routing without going into Cubase's VST Connections window, where these changes are normally made. When opening a new project in Cubase, you'll have the option to select from several templates for the MR816 routing. The most basic template routes inputs 1–8 to audio tracks 1–8. Quick Connect lets you change this routing with literally the touch of a button. Simply select the track you want to record on in Cubase, and then push the Quick Connect button above the channel on the MR816 that you want to route to. That's it—connection made!

TIP

If you want to send an MR816 input to more than one track for recording, simply select the tracks in Cubase and press the Quick Connect button on the desired input channel. This will route that input channel to all of the selected Cubase tracks simultaneously.

This is an example of the hardware controlling the software. Conversely, if you make any routing changes from within the VST Connections window in Cubase, you'll also see those changes take place on the front panel of the MR816.

DSP

The MR816 houses DSP in the form of the REV-X Reverb (MR816X and MR816CSX) and the Morphing Sweet Spot Channel Strip (MR816CSX only). This powerful DSP takes advantage of the tightly integrated hardware and software in that it can be controlled via the hardware controls on the MR816 as well as from a VST plug-in within Cubase.

REV-X REVERB

The REV-X Reverb is a high-quality reverb algorithm from Yamaha, the same one that is built into its professional audio processors and digital mixers. REV-X supplies hall, plate, and room reverb types that can be applied via the MR Editor for stand-alone use, or from within Cubase for monitoring during tracking and as a VST plug-in for mixing (see Fig. 6.5).

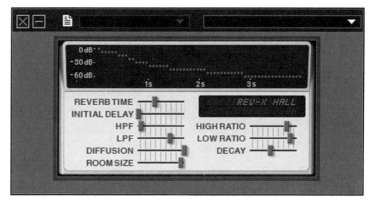

Fig. 6.5: The REV-X Reverb control panel

Accessing REV-X with the MR Editor is very straightforward. The main mixer screen of the MR Editor contains a send for each input channel in the input section as well as a reverb type select window, editor, and time and return controls (see Fig. 6.4). You can set up your reverb parameters and routing here and save them as a preset in the MR Editor, which will save it to the MR816 as well. Now the next time you turn it on, it will remember these settings.

To control the REV-X reverb time and return level on the MR816 hardware, press Control Knob 1 until the REV-X LED is lit. Now, Control Knob 1 adjusts the reverb time and Control Knob 2 adjusts the return level. Adjustments to these controls will be mirrored in real time in the MR Editor or in Cubase, whichever you're using at the time.

There are two ways to access the REV-X for mixing and monitoring with Cubase 5. The first is through the Cubase 5 mixer. REV-X can be used in the same way as the built-in VST effects in Cubase, but running it from the MR816 saves valuable computer CPU resources. To do this, you need to set the MR816 to be used as an external effect.

POWER TIP
Using the MR8I6 REV-X Reverb as an External Effect in Cubase

1. Go to the Device menu in Cubase and select Device Setup…

2. Select the Yamaha Steinberg FW ASIO driver and open the Control Panel.

3. Click on the MR816 tab.

4. Under Settings, pull down the Digital I/O, External FX menu and select the configuration you want to use.

5. Close the Device Setup dialog box.

Now, when you're in the Cubase 5 mixer, the MR816 will show up as an insert effect alongside the built-in VST effects, and is saved with the project so you won't have to reconfigure it again the next time you work on the project.

NOTE
The digital inputs on the MR816 will be disabled when using the unit as an external effect in Cubase 5. If you wish, you can simply enable the digital I/O when tracking and then switch to external effect mode when mixing.

The second way to access the REV-X Reverb on the MR816 is through the Control Room feature of Cubase, which is used for monitoring during recording and overdubbing. Control Room is a powerful mix engine inside Cubase that lets you create monitor mixes for use in a studio situation with no latency. With the MR816, two independent monitor mixes can be created with Control Room, mixed in the hardware using the built-in effects, and monitored through the two headphone outputs.

POWER TIP
Creating Two Monitor Mixes with REV-X Reverb in Control Room

1. Go to the Devices menu in Cubase and select VST Connections.

2. Click the Studio tab and enable Control Room.

3. Click on the Add Channel button and select Add Studio twice to create two new monitor mixes.

4. Under Audio Device, assign the Yamaha Steinberg FW ASIO driver to both mixes created, assign the outputs under Device port, and close the dialog box.

5. Go to the Device menu in Cubase and select Control Room Mixer (you will see your two mixes appear, turned on and set to AUX).

6. Go to the main Mixer window in Cubase and extend the view.

7. Click the Show Studio Sends (you can adjust each mix to taste here).

8. Open the Input Mixer and extend the view to show the MR816 input settings.

9. Adjust the amount of reverb desired for each channel.

10. Go to the Device menu in Cubase and select Audio Hardware Setup for the MR816.

11. Select your monitor setups as the source for headphones 1 and 2, adjust the REV-X Reverb levels, and close the dialog box.

You now have two different monitor mixes for headphones 1 and 2, with independent amounts of REV-X reverb. The overall level of these can be adjusted from the MR816 front panel multicontrol knobs by clicking the first knob until the Phones LED is lighted. Each mix can be adjusted to the individual performer's taste using the Studio sends in the Cubase mixer.

Because setting up the monitor mixes is somewhat of a process, it's a good idea to set these up and save them with your template so they will be available when you start a new project.

SWEET SPOT MORPHING CHANNEL STRIP

The Sweet Spot Morphing Channel Strip comes from a Yamaha algorithm designed to make complicated compression and EQ settings quick and easy (see Fig. 6.6). It does this by starting with several presets that were conceived by top studio engineers. These presets include compression and EQ settings for a variety of inputs such as vocals, drums, and bass guitar. They can be called up on the MR816 by pressing Control Knob 1 until the Morph LED is lit. Then you use Control Knob 1 to "morph" through various presets and Control Knob 2 to adjust the amount of drive.

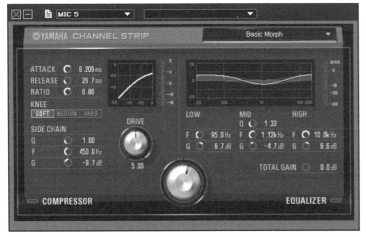

Fig. 6.6: The Sweet Spot Morphing Channel Strip control panel

While the idea of the Sweet Spot Morphing Channel Strip is to make compression and EQ easy and fast, the underlying technology is very complicated, and can be further controlled in detail. After all, it's called a channel strip because it includes a fully functioning compressor and EQ with all the bells and whistles. This makes for a best-of-both-worlds approach. If you're a beginning user, you can start with the presets to get some great results as well as tweak them using the Morph and Drive functions. While doing this, you'll not only notice how the sound changes, but you can watch the parameters change in the control panel and see what changes are being made to produce that sound. If you're a pro, the presets are a great starting point to get something up fast. From there you can tweak every aspect of the channel strip if you like by using it in external effect mode within Cubase and adjusting the parameters from the control panel.

In practice, the Sweet Spot Morphing Channel Strip is used in the same ways I described above using the REV-X Reverb. It can also be accessed in the same ways: through the MR Editor, through the Cubase mixer, and through the Control Room function. In fact, you can go through the Power Tip "Using the REV-X Reverb as an External Effect" and simply replace "REV-X" with "Sweet Spot Morphing Channel Strip." The Sweet Spot Morphing Channel Strip can also be used in the Control Room and be applied to monitor signals in the same way that REV-X can. Go through the Power Tip "Creating Two Monitor Mixes with REV-X Reverb in Control Room" and substitute "Sweet Spot Morphing Channel Strip" for "REV-X Reverb."

The MR816 Control Panel

Fig. 6.7: The MR816 control panel

Lastly, the MR816 has a small, dedicated control panel where some of the general settings can be adjusted (see Fig. 6.7). This control panel can be accessed through the Device Setup menu in Cubase through the Yamaha Steinberg FW ASIO driver.

The Yamaha Steinberg FW ASIO driver dialog has three tabs: The General tab is where you set the sample rate, word clock master, and clock source as well as the ASIO driver settings and WDM driver settings. The MR816X or MR816CSX tab contains the firmware version and lets you select your digital IO and effects settings. The About tab simply states the driver version number. Check here when you need to update.

CC121 ADVANCED INTEGRATION CONTROLLER

The CC121 Advanced Integration Controller is the other piece of hardware to come from the first round of joint Yamaha/Steinberg development. It too is a great example of how tight integration "hooks" the hardware into the software for easier and faster workflow. The CC121 is a dedicated remote control for Cubase. In fact, the model number stands for "Cubase Control One-to-One," meaning that each control is dedicated to one function inside Cubase. While a simple concept, this eliminates the learning curve as well as the endless paging through menus that is required on many "generic" controllers, greatly increasing the speed of your work.

The CC121 is a desktop unit measuring about 11 inches wide by 7 inches deep with an angled top. It fits very comfortably on a desktop next to a laptop or other gear. (It also matches my silver MacBook Pro very nicely.) It's even small enough to fit on many keyboard controllers if you're inclined to work that way. The unit is USB bus–powered, although in order to activate the touch-sensitive motorized fader, you'll need to connect the AC power adapter. The CC121 comes with a CD that contains the CC121 Extension for Cubase and a USB-MIDI driver.

Getting Around the CC121

The top of the CC121 is divided into thirds, with the middle third set apart in a black box (see Fig. 6.8). This is done to help you quickly identify areas that correspond to certain functions. I've found that setting the CC121 up to the left of my MacBook with a mouse on the right lets me use both hands together in a very effective way. Most of the adjustments on the CC121 are made via button pushes and knob turns, which become comfortable to do fairly quickly with my less-coordinated hand (I'm right-handed) while my right hand can do the fine-motor-skill mouse work.

The left-hand third of the CC121 is dedicated to the Channel Strip in Cubase. Here, you'll find a 100 mm touch-sensitive motorized fader, a pan knob, dedicated track controls for mute, solo, read and write automation, monitor, record, edit channel

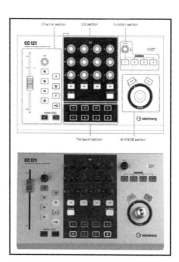

Fig. 6.8: CC121 Advanced Integration Controller

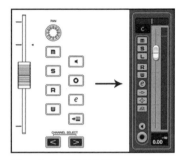

Fig. 6.9: CC121 Channel Strip and Cubase Channel Strip

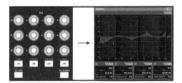

Fig. 6.10: CC121 EQ section and Cubase EQ section

and edit instrument, as well as Channel Select buttons. In pursuing the goal of dedicated control, Steinberg gave the track control buttons the same icons you'll see on the Cubase screen, and they even appear in the same color (see Fig. 6.9). Using the Channel Select buttons that are strategically located at the bottom, closest to your hand, you can quickly cursor through tracks and make fader, pan, and other adjustments very quickly, as well as write automation as you go. It works very well for mixing.

The middle third of the CC121, inside the black box, features the EQ section on the top and the transport section at the bottom. The EQ section is a matrix set up to correspond to the EQ section you see in Cubase. There are four columns of three knobs in the matrix. These knobs correspond to the frequency from left to right: low, low-mid, high-mid, and high, while the top row controls the Q, the middle row controls the frequency, and the bottom row controls the gain. Under each column is an On/Off button, and under these are EQ Type and All Bypass buttons. When you call up the EQ section on a track in Cubase, you can see in real time any adjustments you make in the EQ section (see Fig. 6.10).

Under the EQ section are the transport controls. Again, these are strategically placed closest to your hand and in the middle of the unit, as they are most likely going to be the controls you use most often.

The right-hand third of the unit contains assignable Function controls 1–4 at the top and the unique AI knob at the bottom. The Function controls are, by default, set up to work with the Control Room feature of Cubase 5. If Control Room is active and it's in Studio Control mode, then the Function buttons correspond to Studio 1–4 and the knob controls the output gain. If you're in Monitor Control mode, then the Function buttons correspond to Monitor 1–4 while the knob controls their output gain.

You can also assign the Function buttons and knob to perform certain key commands or adjust certain parameters. This can also be done with the footswitch on the back of the unit.

POWER TIP
Assigning Custom Functions on the CC121

1. Go to the Device menu in Cubase and select Device Setup…

2. Under Remote Devices, select CC121.

3. Under User Commands, assign your desired commands to the Function 1–4 buttons and footswitch (if connected).

4. Under the Custom Assignment pull-down menu, select from the list which parameter you want to control with the knob: Metronome Level, Main Mix Level, Control Room Level, or Control Room Headphones.

5. Click OK.

Now, you'll have custom commands and parameter adjustments assigned to the Function section. These assignments will be saved with the project, and it is a good idea to save them with your templates so you'll have them each time you start a project. If you want to change back to the default Control Room functions, go back into the Device Setup dialog and click Reset.

At the bottom of the right-hand third of the CC121 is the large AI knob. To me, this is the most unique, and possibly the biggest time-saving, function on the entire unit. Again, AI stands for Advanced Integration, and this is where it shows. Simply hover your mouse over any control in Cubase or any VST3 plug-in, and turn the AI knob to adjust it. You don't need to click on the control, just hover the mouse over it and turn the knob. This is an extremely fast way to work with VST effects, VST instruments, and other areas of Cubase where you need to adjust parameter values. I've gotten very fast at hovering the mouse with my right hand and adjusting the values via the AI knob with my left hand. The parameters adjusted with the AI knob can also be automated. Just make sure that Write automation is enabled and you're working within Cubase 5 or a VST3 plug-in.

The AI knob also has two other functions. Engaging the Jog button turns the AI knob into a Jog/Shuttle wheel for Cubase. This is great for locating specific points during audio editing. The Lock button will lock the AI knob on its current function.

This is handy if you hover the mouse over a parameter and you want the AI knob to keep controlling that parameter while you do something else with the mouse.

The Fader

A 100 mm touch-sensitive motorized fader is a highly sought after tool for mixing. Much of the cost of high-end mixing consoles is due to the quality of their faders. This is where an engineer puts his or her touch on a mix. And as different people have different "feel" for a fader, you can adjust the sensitivity of the CC121 fader to suit your taste.

POWER TIP
Adjusting the Touch-Sensitivity of the CC121 Fader

1. Turn the CC121 and the computer off.

2. Connect the CC121 to the computer.

3. Start the computer.

4. While pressing both Channel Select buttons, turn the CC121 on.

5. The sensitivity of the fader is indicated by how many track control buttons are lighted from bottom to top, or 1–8 (see Fig. 6.11).

6. To set a higher sensitivity, select more track control buttons (up to all 8); to lower the sensitivity, deselect more track control buttons (down to 1).

7. Try the fader and repeat step 6 to set the desired sensitivity.

8. Turn the unit off to save.

Sensitivity	Button
8	[M] (Mute) button
7	[◄] (Monitor) button
6	[S] (Solo) button
5	[O] (Enable Record) button
4	[R] (Read Enable) button
3	[e] (Channel Settings) button
2	[W] (Write Enable) button
1	[→▥] (Edit Instrument) button

Fig. 6.11: CC121 fader sensitivity levels

INSIDER
Steinberg Product Marketing Manager
Stefan Schreiber Discusses Hardware and
Software Integration

How does the relationship with Yamaha work when developing hardware?

We are always exchanging our internal ideas, customer ideas, and customer reports to make the products better. Since there is no product planner for hardware at Steinberg, I also do some parts of product planning, so I'm a bit more on the technical side and have more communication with Yamaha in that regard.

We discuss how we can best implement and integrate [various proposals]. We try to find out what the best combination of hardware and software would be, and how we can provide the best solution. We talk about this a long, long time, so the hardware design changes a lot during this planning. And of course we, on the Steinberg side, have to figure out what has to be done in Cubase; what the hardware can mean to Cubase and what would be good, user-friendly specs and features. There is always a very intense discussion and exchange of ideas, and then at the end it becomes more concrete, and we have a product.

What are some of the design goals when collaborating with Yamaha?

One general idea is that you can control the hardware from within the software, and you can control some aspects of the software from the hardware. This is true of the CC121 of course, but I'm talking more about the MR. With other hardware you need to use a mouse to make your connections in the software, and now you can make them by just clicking a knob and everything is created. So there is interaction between hardware and software, and there is a much easier workflow. I think this is one fundamental goal.

Also, tight integration with Cubase with the DSP effects, routing for the monitoring, and the headphone mixes are a big goal. Again, you can control these from either the hardware or the software. This is very nice for the user, because they always have direct access to Cubase. It's always two-way communication; everything you see in the hardware you will see in the software, and everything you do in the software you will see in the hardware.

One of the interesting things about the workflow, the ease of configuration, is that for the professional user it means that they can work faster. Or for someone who is buying an interface for the first time, it's going to be easier for them to get going. Quick Connect, for example, is a unique way of working. No other interface can do that with software. It's exciting to see where this will go. We already have the next two products in development, so it's just a starting point.

How about the look of the products?

This is a collaboration between Steinberg and Yamaha. There are some functional design aspects of the new products that work very well. The curved front edge of the CC121, for example, is very easy on the wrist, especially if it's sitting up higher where sharp corners on tabletop gear can be uncomfortable.

We also didn't skimp on the quality of the components. There was some discussion about the CC121 and its price point. For one fader, it can be seen as expensive, but looking at the quality of the components; the metal casing; a very high-end, touch-sensitive fader; and so on, it's a really good value. The CC121 is designed to be a real workhorse. For people working eight hours a day, this unit should work for years and years. It's a nice design, but it is also sturdy and very ergonomic.

And you can update the hardware with firmware between new products?

Yes. I'm on the forums and talking with our product specialists and listening to what customers are saying. I report this back to Yamaha, and we have a look at what can be solved via firmware. This way we can not only fix problems, but also add features that people want. We are constantly working to enhance the workflow of the products.

What is the biggest challenge in developing new hardware?

I think the biggest challenge is the integration and the workflow between the hardware and software. It sounds quite easy, but many customers are used to the way hardware and software worked in the past, so when we make the workflow easier, it is still a change for them. For example, with the MR816, customers asked us where the mixing application is to run between the hardware and Cubase. This is a common thing with many hardware manufacturers. We don't have this because you don't need it. You have to convince customers to change the way they think about integration to improve it. I don't think people are used to tight integration yet. RME has a mixing application, M-Audio has one, and so on. This was necessary because the software was out of the hardware manufacturer's control. Customers know how to work with this, even though it isn't the best workflow. Customers get confused, for example, as to why the MR editor doesn't open when they are working in Cubase. And the reason is that there is no need for it. Cubase does everything and the MR talks directly to it.

CUBASE IC

The iPhone has become a juggernaut for development for companies in just about any market you can imagine. At the time I'm writing this, Apple says it has surpassed 50,000 apps for download in the App Store and more than a billion downloads since the launch of the iPhone. These are impressive numbers that are surely much, much higher as you read this. Steinberg has harnessed the power of the iPhone platform with a free app called Cubase iC, a remote control for the iPhone and iPod Touch (see Fig. 6.12). Cubase iC's main function is as a remote

Fig. 6.12: Steinberg Cubase iC transport screen

transport control, but it also gives you access to the Arranger track, which in addition to being fun and creative, can be used as a live performance tool.

In order to use Cubase iC, you'll first need a wireless network running on your Cubase 5 computer. Then you'll need to download the free Cubase iC app from the iTunes App Store. Then, go to the Steinberg website (www.steinberg.net) and download the Steinberg SKI Remote, an extension that allows it to run with Cubase 5.

Once you've downloaded the app and Steinberg SKI Remote, launch Cubase 5 and then launch Cubase iC on an iPhone or iPod Touch. In Cubase iC, touch the Connection tab at the bottom of the front screen and touch Connect. You will now see your Cubase 5 and host computer in the list of hosts. Select it by touching it.

Now, touch the Transport tab and you will be able to have transport control of Cubase from anywhere within the range of your wireless network. The Transport tab give you access to location with two locator strips across the top. Under these locator strips are standard transport controls. And under the transport controls you'll find icons for Arranger On/Off, Metronome Click On/Off, Precount On/Off, and Cycle On/Off.

The Arranger Track

Fig. 6.13: Steinberg Cubase iC Arranger screen

If you use the Arranger track in Cubase 5, you can access it by touching the Arranger tab in Cubase iC (see Fig. 6.13). Here, you will see the Arranger buttons as they appear in Cubase. You can create real-time arrangements by touching the buttons during playback as well as control the jump to the next section.

Suggested uses for Cubase iC:

1. To record yourself while playing an instrument like a guitar or when you're behind a drum kit.

2. To control Cubase from an isolation booth to record vocals.

3. To control Cubase from different listening positions in your studio or room.

4. As an arranging tool for live performance.

5. To control Cubase on stage to run backing tracks.

6. To work out arrangements with a band in rehearsal.

COPY PROTECTION

It may seem strange to talk about copy protection along with the new features in Cubase 5, but there have been some developments in Steinberg's business model that may help you see copy protection in a different light and work it to your advantage, rather than see it as a hindrance.

In the interview with Steinberg founder Charlie Steinberg near the end of this book, he talks about the company's need for copy protection from the beginning, because it was difficult for people to see a value in software as opposed to hardware. Software was simply seen as a floppy disk and some packaging worth a few dollars. With the ability to quickly and easily make copies, it would have become hard for Steinberg to maintain its software development. Yet it was very difficult for Steinberg to convey the value of software development, the people behind it, and its intellectual property. There were people with ideas and technical skills that needed to be employed, as well as capital investment like equipment and an office.

The need for copy protection still exists today. In addition to the value battle, which still wages on, the Internet makes it easy to distribute illegal copies of software worldwide. Also, following the fight over file-sharing websites and the changing distribution of digital music over the past few years, an entire generation of consumers has entered the market believing that things like music, movies, and software should be freely distributed, or at least very inexpensive. There are other aspects that play into software piracy—like the desire to try software before you buy it—but ultimately any form of piracy is not good for further software development, not to mention the fact that it's simply stealing.

Ray Williams, founder of the International Music Software Trade Association (IMSTA), an advocacy group against illegal software piracy, once told me that he sees three distinct groups of software consumer: those who will always buy and register every piece of software they use, those who will always pirate software if they can, and those who will do some of both. The "some of both" group may want to try it, can't afford it, or may justify pirating it in other ways. Unfortunately, evidence shows the last two groups to be the largest, forcing companies like Steinberg to spend time and money on the development of copy protection.

Bringing Copy Protection In-House

In recent years Steinberg has taken steps to not only make copy protection more effective, but also more transparent. The company uses the Syncrosoft USB e-Licenser and management system, which consists of a USB "key" or "dongle," which holds the licenses for all of your installed Steinberg products and is maintained through a management application (see Fig. 6.14). The USB key, as Steinberg calls it, comes with Cubase or can be purchased as a separate product if you want to use Steinberg plug-ins with another DAW package.

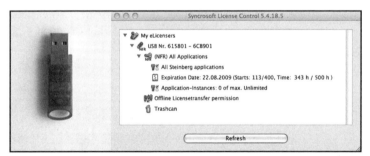

Fig. 6.14: Steinberg USB e-Licenser and control software

In early 2009, Steinberg acquired the USB e-Licenser and copy protection management IP from Syncrosoft, bringing the entire copy protection system in-house. This means that Steinberg now has full control over its development and implementation, and can work even further toward the goal of making copy protection effective and transparent as it integrates it further into its products.

INSIDER
Steinberg Managing Director Andreas Stelling on the Acquisition of Syncrosoft IP

Tell us about this acquisition.

We did not acquire Syncrosoft as a company. We acquired IP (intellectual property), which in this case was the license management IP and the license for the copy protection system. We were not the only customer of Syncrosoft, so we will provide this solution to other third parties, like Arturia, Korg, Vienna, and so on.

Our goal is to make copy protection easier to use, to make it more integrated into our products. We make the keys, we generate the licenses, and we will develop the applications further. We can make sure the right priorities are set. It's much easier to do this when it's in-house. For example, we have developed software to make it easier to make the USB keys. In the past they were handmade, and subcomponents were shipped back and forth, and we thought that was not a good idea. We have optimized that process.

We also wanted to be independent of Syncrosoft, because if we were to lose the ability to maintain the copy protection system, with the size of our user base it would be a disaster. It was a bit of a risk-minimizing acquisition.

You must have a lot of confidence in this copy-protection system to have acquired it.

We need to show our customers that there is a benefit in license management. I have these arguments about copy protection and whether it is needed. The good news is that Cubase 4 was the first version that has never been cracked, and we are pretty confident that Cubase 5 will not be cracked, so it's kind of evidence that the copy-protection system we have in place is working well.

Is piracy still a big challenge?

Yes. Copy protection is still important for us, because it is saving people's jobs here. If you have a cracked version and it's easy to get, then many people will not buy [the software]. There are always arguments for what would happen if you don't have copy protection. Will more people buy it because there are more copies out for people to try? We have hundreds of thousands of OEM versions out in the market, so whatever hardware you buy, you usually get an OEM version of Cubase with it. So, you don't need to have a cracked version. It's available to almost anyone.

Cubase in Studio Recording

7

Since its early years as a MIDI sequencer, Cubase has been employed in countless studio recording sessions around the world. Over the years, it has migrated from its MIDI roots to become the centerpiece of entire professional recording facilities, handling tracking, monitoring, editing, and mixing. Cubase has been used on Grammy Award–winning records and chart-topping hits, and continues to grow as a professional recording platform.

In this chapter, we'll hear from three recording professionals that rely on Cubase day in and day out to complete their work. We'll hear how Cubase is incorporated into their studios and workflow, and pick up some tips along the way.

STEVE LAMM— CRYPTIC GLOBE RECORDING (CGR STUDIOS)
Nashville, TN

Steve Lamm is a Nashville-based studio owner, recording engineer, and session guitar player. Steve's musical and technical skills bring him diverse work in studio recording, live recording, songwriting, producing, session work, and even building custom DAW systems for other audio professionals in the Nashville area.

He won a 2009 Grammy Award in the category of Best Rock or Rap Gospel Album for his work as a recording engineer on Toby Mac's *Alive and Transported*.

How long have you been using Cubase?

I got into Cubase when I switched from a Soundcraft Ghost console and an ADAT in the early '90s. Back then I think it was Cubase VST24. I tried all of the different things that were available at the time: Logic, Pro Tools, and Cakewalk before it was Sonar. Cubase made the most sense to me. As I looked at recording music and having done it on analog gear, Cubase just seemed like it was laid out better. It just made sense to me. I could open it up and immediately start to work without reading the manual. And that has stuck with me through all the revisions.

Cubase VST really had an analog studio look and feel. Was that the attraction?

VST24 is where I came in, and yeah, the graphical interface has always been a big part of it. It looks like what I would expect that hardware to look like. Here's the mixer and here's the recorder, here's the EQ, the inserts, and all of that. Graphically it's always made a lot of sense. I'm a huge Dave Nicholson [Steinberg GUI architect; see chapter 5] fan!

It's also the layout. The signal flow and how you route things. When you open up Logic, it takes you 10 minutes to figure out how to create an audio track and route audio to it. With Cubase, I didn't have that problem as a new user. Now, granted, I've been doing it for a long, long time now, and this is my main DAW software, so I must admit some bias as far as the ease of use. Still, when I show people how to use it, which I do regularly, it's very, very simple. You fire it up, create a new project, and you're working almost instantly, with no training at all.

What is the main type of work you use Cubase for?

I use it for a lot of different things. My work is varied. The list would include location recording, which is what I won a Grammy for this year, where we actually go on site and record in the venues. In this particular case it was down in Houston, where we recorded tobyMac. I have a mobile rig that has a PC in it and converters and preamps, and we roll that in and record the band on location.

I also have CGR Studios here in Nashville. Here, Cubase and Nuendo are the host software for the commercial studio, which sometimes I'm engineering and sometimes I'm not. I also do my own production work and produce artists, as well as play guitar on other people's projects. And lastly, I use Cubase for songwriting.

Can you describe what your studio setup is like for the various kinds of work that you do?

For each task, I have some basic templates set up as far as the software is concerned. As far as the hardware is concerned, for the location recording system I have two racks. The first rack houses the computer and the converters. Currently, I'm using an RME MADI card into the RME ADI6432 MADI-to-AES converter, which goes to 48 channels of Lynx converters. This is connected to the other rack, which has the preamps in it via Elco snakes. The preamp rack has a variety of preamps: Vintech, Seventh Circle Audio, API, DBX, and pre's like that. We generally rent for the rest of the channels, and I've been using ATI preamps, which are made by API and are really great. So, I'll fill the racks up with those, and then they all connect with Elco cables for a quick in and out.

The back of the rack is XLR, and we just plug in the split from the front-of-house mixer. They usually supply the split, and when they don't, I rent one. We just plug right into the back of the rack, and we're getting the same feed from the microphones on stage that front of house and the monitors are getting.

I have a template set up in the software so I can roll in and be ready to record in about 20 minutes. It's really quick and easy. And these racks are pretty cool. When the front lids come off they become a table for my keyboard, mouse, and monitors. All I need is a chair!

Do you monitor with headphones or speakers?

I've got a PreSonus Central Station and bring headphones and Event 20/20p's with me. Generally, we're set up in a room that's pretty far removed from the stage, so we have decent separation and I can actually hear what's going on in my monitors.

How about your setup in the studio?

Actually, it's almost exactly the same rig. I've got those two racks set up to connect via Elco cables to the patchbay in my studio. The rig rolls right back into the studio, and I pop the front and back off, plug in the Elcos and the power, and I'm back in the studio business.

Currently we have a custom desk that we had Custom Consoles build for us. The desk has a brand-new Toft ATB32 console in it, which we mainly use for the EQs on the front end. And then the Euphonix Artists Series controllers are all housed in the same desk, with a big patchbay and some outboard gear.

When we roll back in, the patchbay interfaces all the preamps, converters, and everything, and everything is normaled, so you generally don't even have to use the patchbay for a basic session. The mic ties go right into the mic pre's and the pre outputs go into the line in of the Toft so you can use the EQ. Then the direct out of the Toft goes into the converters and the output of the converters goes right to the headphone system — they're normaled to that. So everything is already set up. You can, of course, mix and match, throw compressors in and all that sort of stuff, because everything has a point on the patchbay.

And again, I have a template set up in the software for the studio, so when someone wants to come in and track, I just call up a template and all they have to do is select which channel they want to put in record.

When do you use Nuendo instead of Cubase?

The only reason I'm using Nuendo right now is because I use a PC exclusively and I don't have any Euphonix support for Cubase 5 yet. It does work with Nuendo on PC as long as you have a Mac on the network, which I do — a little Mac Mini.

Depending on the client, I run Nuendo if it's not someone who's coming in specifically for me, because it still has higher-end name recognition as far as being a Pro Tools competitor. And that's the key word in the industry, Pro Tools, and when people who don't know anything else ask if I run Pro Tools, I say I run Nuendo, and they're fine with it. Cubase is seen differently, which is ridiculous because when it comes to most audio features, they're the same. But I still get that and still run Nuendo for tracking those projects just because they want to see it.

Do you use the Control Room feature in the studio?

Absolutely. I use it exclusively for my headphones. For the talent, I have a template set up and use kind of a hybrid. I have the Furman HDS-16 Headphone Distribution System, which is all analog. I generally create one or two stereo headphone mixes for the talent, and the Furman can have up to four stereo and eight mono, so I'll give them either one or two stereo mixes and then I create the eight monos from the effect sends of the channels. So, send 1 may be just the kick drum, and send 2 will be just the snare, 3 will be bass guitar, and 4 will be just the electric guitar. That way, they can create their own mix.

I've been bugging the guys at Steinberg to allow me to do that from Control Room, to have eight stereos and at least eight monos from the control room section. That's how everybody's working these days in all the commercial studios. In fact, in most studios, they give the talent the same mixes as the control room and then they give them the "more me" to add to it if they need to hear more of themselves. We take it a step further and actually give them a mix that they all approve of and then let them tweak it for more or less of this or that.

It makes it easy in my templates because I pull it up and I'm pretty much ready to go. I don't generally have to adjust much. I almost never get requests for headphone changes anymore. We're doing that with an Intel I7-based system now at very low latency, so we can offer reverb right in the box. In situations where I've got a lot going on, effects or whatever, and I need to overdub, I just switch over to direct monitoring, which is now supported in Control Room. Now if they would just make the effect sends supported in Control Room like direct monitoring, we'd be set!

What are you favorite features in Cubase 5?

A feature I really like in Cubase 5 is Record Lock. It's a new key command that lets you lock the record-enable, and the only way you can take it out of record is by using the mouse. If you push a button to take it out of record, it gives you an "Are you sure?" message, and you have to click on it with the mouse to actually come out. This is great for location recording. Sometimes when you're flying around the screen and you accidentally hit the space bar, it can knock it out of record. That's a great feature.

I also love the Batch Export feature because most of the labels are asking for delivery in stems now. It's also wonderful for delivery to people that are doing the next step in a project in another software application. So, if I'm tracking drums, bass, and guitar here and then it's going to somebody else to track vocals using Pro Tools, I can just export the track and any edits with a Batch Export and I can tell it what folder to go to and it's done. It makes it really nice in a world where we still don't have a working unified format for project exchange.

Is there anything you'd like to see in the next version of Cubase?

To me the only thing Cubase is missing at this point is a really well-working multitrack drum editor that would compete with Digidesign's Beat Detective. That's something that has been asked for since Beat Detective came out. I actually sent Steinberg a long thesis on how they could do it by taking existing features and making a sort of macro out of them. I'm sure what they come up with will be amazing. They have told me that they have not forgotten about it and still have it in the works.

Have you developed any techniques of your own to help you with Cubase?

I have quite a few custom key commands, which I map to an X-keys USB input device. It's a generic keypad, and you can make your own labels for it. Each key can be programmed to be any set of keystrokes. So, I'll create my own custom key commands, and then I assign them to a button on the X-Key and label it. That way, I don't even have to remember what the key command is, and other engineers and producers also have access to them just by looking at the keypad. It allows me to make it very customizable for myself, but also for others that might not be so familiar with the program. Everyone can get to it very easily.

BRENT BODRUG—B-GROUP MUSIC
Toronto, Canada

Producer/engineer/songwriter Brent Bodrug has found commercial success writing songs with major-label artists as well as producing countless independent artists with his own production company, B-Group Music. An accomplished jazz pianist who studied under the great Oscar Peterson, Brent brings his writing, arranging, and performing skills into the studio to produce up-and-coming acts. He recently moved into a new recording space, converting a century-old church into a world-class recording studio. Here, we discuss his use of Cubase and how he has developed some interesting ways of working with it over the years.

What version of Cubase are you using?

Cubase 4.52 on a PC. I have a MacBook as well, but my main rig is running Windows XP.

It seems some people upgrade slowly, especially when a system is very stable for them, and others need to be on the bleeding edge all the time.

I was that way in my 20s. I was buying a new Mac every six months, and I would wait for the night that the next download was going to be available and go get it, or go to the store the day I knew they had it. But I find if I stay one version behind, it's generally good for me. I'll go to Cubase 5 when it gets to 5.1. The other reason is that I need to upgrade my computer, and I'm not anxious to upgrade that.

It's interesting, because when the computers weren't powerful enough to run the software really efficiently, it was all about upgrading. But these days I have a very modest PC, a good one by today's specs, but it's certainly not a very fast machine. It's a single Xeon processor, and I can run a 60- or 70-track mix on it with no problems. Certainly things would get faster if I were to get a faster machine, but I don't really find that the overhead is much of a problem.

Tell me about the work that you do.

I tend to fit into the mold of what the new producer/engineer guys are these days. I have my own studio, which is actually quite good. I recently bought an old church and converted it into a studio, so I've got a nice, big, live space for folks that want to record live. I tend to attract mostly independent artists these days. I've also done some things with some label acts and lots of writing camps for publishers and stuff, but these days what I tend to do are projects where I'm co-writing with artists or I'll workshop their songs with them. Then we'll do preproduction rehearsals, and once we're satisfied that everything is good, then we'll go on to recording. If it's a solo artist, I'll find a good group of players. I've got a big network of musicians. And then after the fact I usually help out with connecting them with other bands or publishing people or record people.

So, you're really taking a band or an artist all the way through the writing and recording process.

Yeah, and sometimes there is more emphasis on certain things. Right now I'm working with these two 14-year-old girls that don't really have any experience with any aspect of it, but are just really talented vocalists. So with them I tend to do a lot more writing, and finding the players, and I'm sort of the captain of the ship a little bit more. On the other hand, I just had a band in here that had me locked out for two weeks, and they had a very specific idea of the tones they liked and the arrangements, and the tunes were pretty worked out, so in that case I was more of an engineer.

I also do a lot of songwriting demos where I'm programming using virtual instruments and stuff. I started as a programmer, and my background was MIDI in the beginning. I was one of the early guys into having the computer running sequencing software and slaving it to a tape machine to do vocals and stuff. I used to do a lot of full arrangements that way. And as it's evolved I've gotten more and more into the audio side.

Being an early MIDI guy, when do you start using Cubase?

I started using Cubase when it first went to VST. It's interesting: I started on the Atari with Notator, and when the Atari went away I went to the Mac and was using Logic. And I just found Logic a little too deep menu-wise for me back then. I found the software was getting in the way, and a good friend of mine at a dealer in Toronto said I had to check out Cubase. The very first version of VST had come out, and he said, "Give me 20 minutes and you'll walk out with the software." Sure enough, that's what happened! I went in for 20 minutes and he showed me what I could do, and it was sort of the culmination of the dream for me as a programmer guy. I didn't have to deal with SMPTE or locking stuff up, I could just have everything on one screen in one place. At that point I walked out of the store with it, learned how to use it, and I've been working in it ever since.

VST hit in 1996. That brought a lot of people to Cubase.

Yeah, it was heads and shoulders above everything else. I had friends who had Sound Tools, and it was like two-track audio, and it just seemed ridiculous to me. To be honest, I've felt that way all along. Cubase always seems to be ahead of the curve. Cubase has its issues, but certainly Steinberg seems to be on the leading edge of the new technologies and at the forefront of what's happening. It's funny because these days you have to spend equal amounts of time in Pro Tools as well if you travel around. So, you spend some time in Pro Tools and people think it's cutting edge, but Cubase has had things for years that they're just starting to get now.

Tell me about the new studio.

It's an old church. It's got 14-foot ceilings and the live space is about 1,000 square feet with nice hardwood floors and everything. And then my control room is another 500 or 600 square feet. I'm in the process of putting a couple of isolation booths into the live space. The control room will be divided so that it has a vocal booth, so there will be three isolation rooms, a control room, and a live space.

I've got three drum kits, 25 guitar amps, and about 20 guitars, a Hammond organ, a piano, and all the old electric pianos, a Minimoog, an Arp Odyssey, and bunch of MIDI gear. I've got a PA in there for when we rehearse. The basement of the church is an apartment where folks can stay.

How is your Cubase system set up?

I've got a really nice front end. I've got a Millennia Origin, Amek, Focusrite, Great River, Daking, Vintech—a lot of it sort of reminiscent of Neve stuff. I've got some really nice compression, a Universal Audio 1176, a Smart C2, which is like an SSL, a Crane Song Trakker, and some Joe Meek stuff.

I use a Presonus Central Station as my monitoring system. I sold my console a while ago because I wasn't using it anymore. I mix in the box 100 percent now, and the Central Station is just like the master section of a console where you can have a talkback and select different sets of speakers.

What are you using for I/O?

I got Mytek 8x96s, which are real nice. I've got an Apogee Rosetta 200 and a Digi 003 for when I have to use Pro Tools. I also have a MOTU 308 box, which is basically just digital I/O, but all my conversion comes from the Apogee and the Myteks.

For mixing in the box, do you use a controller?

No. I'm a mouse guy, because I've been doing it for so long. I'm a mouse guy and a type guy, actually. One of the things that might be different is the way I mix. I tend to just get good overall levels with the faders in Cubase, but then rather than write automation or have the faders move, I just snip up the tracks into phrases and use the Info Line at the top of the screen to type in however many dB up or down I need it.

When you look at my mix, the fader won't move, but if you look at the track in the Project window it'll be all snipped up, and I'll raise and lower the level depending on the phrase by typing in values. I find it's faster.

Do you do this all at once or as you go along in a project?

Sometimes I do it while I go. If I'm comping a vocal and one take was a little softer than the others, I'll bump it up a little bit while I'm compiling the take. Some of it tends to happen while I'm recording and some happens later. When I'm actually mixing, I set it up with faders and get it so that it's sounding good, and then just listen for parts where something isn't speaking properly. That's where I bump it up or down using the Info Line across the top.

Do you use VST or external effects?

A combination of both. I like the IK Multimedia CSR. I've got the UAD stuff on four cards. I also have PowerCore, which is pretty cool. So I tend to use a combination. I have some old boxes, too. One of my favorite reverbs — and when I tell people this they almost fall off their chair — is an Electro-Harmonix Holy Grail guitar pedal. Lately I've been using it on lead vocals, because it sounds kind of grainy. I just come out of an output and into a Radial X-Amp re-amplifier to bring it down to a reasonable level, run it into the effect, and back into the converter and record it.

Other than that I don't tend to use outboard gear when I'm mixing. Once I'm in the box I stay in. Back in the day I used to play around with sending stuff in and out, but conversion wasn't really up to the quality that it needed to be for it to work well. I think conversion is now good enough to go in and out of the box, but I'm just so used to staying in the box that I only run things out to use the guitar pedals or my old reverb units just because they're a littler thicker and grainier than the stuff in the box. I only do this for specific projects if I'm looking for a specific sound. I can mix a record in the box and be completely happy.

Do you use a lot of virtual instruments in your songwriting work?

Yeah, especially on the songwriting demos, which tend to be more virtual than anything just because of how fast it is. I still don't think most of them are up there sonically yet, and I think there's something to be gained with an old instrument and recording it in through nice gear. You can generally get a sound that will sit better in the mix. But something like M-Tron has become completely indispensable to me. I have Ivory, which I use if I don't have time to mic up my piano. Some of the Native Instruments stuff is good. I use Battery a lot for drums. I'm not crazy about any of the Hammond stuff—I guess because I have a real Hammond—but in a pinch it works, and I've used them on records before. The synthesizers are interesting, and it's certainly nice to be able to program and change the sounds with a good interface. But again, I find them a little two-dimensional, or not quite as big-sounding as I get with other stuff.

Again, for songwriting demos, it's fine. When I'm doing a writing session I have a template that has Battery and Ivory set up, because I'm a piano player. When I pull up the session it's all there and I'm ready to go. I can set the tempo, play a little piano, and we can build it from there. Even though I consider myself a bit of a gear guy, my process for songwriting is very organic. I still tend to write at the piano. I don't like to turn on other instruments until the tune is already written. I'm not one to fire some beats up and write that way. Sometimes I might write with just a guitar and a little handheld recorder. The technology tends to distract me from the actual song. For me, those tools are very much about production. I know this is different than what most people do these days. Most people start with the beat these days. It's an arrangement choice for me—not anything against the technology.

I think for those of us that did this before the technology was as good as it is, it's a process that we're used to. Certainly, I've gone through phases where the technology ruled, and it was all about the beats, but I've found that the writing is better if you just concentrate on the song first, and then the production. It's really easy to get lost in the production and forget about the song. For me, being a traditional guy who likes a good song, I think it's important, and at the end of the day I think most people would agree that a good song shouldn't need all the bells and whistles to be good. You should be able to sit down at the campfire and play it on a guitar, and it should work.

Do you have any favorite techniques that you've come up with using Cubase?

Well there's the mixing in the Info Line thing I mentioned. People have watched me do that and they freak out, because they've never seen anybody work like that, and they're expecting me to push faders, which I rarely do.

The other thing I do, which a lot of people probably do these days, is I tend not to run effects off the main track. When I'm running delays or whatever on a lead vocal, for example, I'll copy the track and edit it so that only specific parts of the track will be sent through the delay. Then I'll set the send on the copied track to be pre-fader so I can bring the fader down to zero and I'll only hear the remnants of what I've edited through the delay. The thing that's cool about this is that now I can filter what I send. I've got a couple of preset EQs that I've made to take all the top end off, so I can send a really dark sound to the delay. So now I can treat my lead vocal as its own thing and have this other track giving me a really nice dark delay on specific phrases.

I'm also very much a print guy. I like to print effects. Once I've got these things set up, I like to export everything and bring it back in. I've had situations where I've had people ask me to recall something that I did back in Cubase SX2, and who knows what I was using back then. So, I tend to archive everything as audio.

I also tend to keep certain plug-in chains for later use. If I'm doing a mix for a session later on and the sounds were gotten in the same way, it gives me a good starting place. I might have a couple of EQs and a compressor set up, and I'll save that as, say, a kick drum channel. Then, if I'm doing a session and use the same drum, I can load that up and start from there.

The other thing I do, which is maybe a little bit weird, is save channels. I have so many different plug-ins, and they all have a unique sound. Like some of the UAD stuff: the Helios EQ is very dirty sounding, and something like their Precision EQ, which is a very clean EQ. So what I've done is save channels with all my EQs, and when I go to mix, rather than guess which EQ I think is going to enhance a track the most, I'll just load up my channel of EQs, play the track in the context of the mix, and I can just turn one on at a time and hear what it's doing. That way I can get to my chains faster and not have to guess. I have similar chains set up for compressor and other stuff, too. I can quickly audition things and make chains based on what I hear. It keeps me from using the same presets for everything and helps me find chains that work for a given situation.

Is there anything you wish Cubase had that it's missing?

Sometimes. It's becoming less of an issue now, but like five years ago at the height of cutting up drums and quantizing everything, I think Steinberg really missed the boat on coming up with a Beat Detective–type solution. I know that there are ways to do it with hitpoints in Cubase, but it was never quite as easy. Now that the drum-editing craze is not as big, it's not as big of a deal, but I really think multitrack drum editing is something they need to address. Even though we don't need to use it all the time, it's a handy thing to have in certain situations.

There are some interface things about Pro Tools which seem quicker at times. Like one of the things I like about Pro Tools for tracking is you can set a fader level, which is your monitor mix, you hit Record and everything goes to that level. And when you take it out of Record, everything goes back to the levels in the mix the way you had it. The Cubase mixer is very static. So, that's a neat little feature I wish they had. Other than a couple of those little things, it's really cool, and I could probably come up with a list of about 200 things in other programs I don't like, so I think they're doing a great job.

RICK DEPOFI—NY NOISE
New York, NY

Rick Depofi is the creative director of NY Noise, a production company located in the heart of New York City. Rick has worked as a producer, engineer, composer, arranger, and musician in music, film, and TV. He has worked with such artists as Shawn Colvin, Joan Osborne, Elvis Costello, Marc Cohn, Natalie Cole, and Janet Jackson. Rick has had several TV commercial successes for companies like American Express, Duracell, Pepsi, Sears, and AT&T, as well as many documentary film-scoring credits.

Are you using Cubase 5 yet?

I have the Cubase 5 box and the MR816CSX here, but I'm in the middle of three records right now, and I don't like to change anything during a record. I don't move until I have to. Cubase 4 has been dead solid for me on OS 10.4 on a Mac.

I actually track in Nuendo, because that platform never, ever crashes on me. I know two other people who do the same thing. Then, after I'm backed up and the musician's split, I open it up in Cubase and I'm off and running.

What kind of work are you doing these days?

We used to be about 80 percent advertising music and scoring for film. Now, it's absolutely flipped over. I'm doing 80 percent records and 20 percent advertising, and a couple of documentary films on the side.

How long have you been using Cubase?

I've been using Cubase, since … when was the beginning? It had to be 1994, maybe.

Cubase VST came out in 1996, but the first version of Cubase was back in 1989.

Well, I was using it before we built our studio, which we built in 1994, so I probably started using it in 1992 or 1993. I left Performer and Sound Designer II behind.

And what attracted you to Cubase?

A friend of mine who is a songwriter was using it, and he showed me a few things. I liked the interface. I just hated Sound Designer and … I can't say I hated Performer, but I wasn't crazy about it. Cubase just looked so much better.

Today, I would say that 90 percent of the people I work with trade files with guest vocalists who sing on these records with file exchange over the Internet. And everybody works in Pro Tools, except for me and a few other people. And whether they show up at the studio or I'm exchanging files, they're like "Cubase? Really?" But I went to a mastering session the other day with Ted Jensen at Sterling, and lo and behold, he was mastering in Nuendo.

Is it easy for you to exchange files with the other systems?

Everything is so seamless now. I'm working on this Rosanne Cash record, and we sent this track and this separate vocal over to Springsteen, who did the duet with her on this, and they're a Pro Tools house. I just tell them, "Here's the vocal at 24-bit; just send me back a WAV or AIFF." It doesn't matter so much. It's more of a concern if somebody wants to come in here and work on a project that's already in Pro Tools. I don't even have it set up here. I have an Mbox, so I can convert files, but other than that, I haven't had any problems.

People ask me all the time why I don't use Pro Tools. And this is why: I want you to take a vocal track and duplicate it, and then put one of those tracks out of phase, and flip the phase on it. What should happen is it should go away, you shouldn't hear anything. If you do that in Cubase, hit the phase switch on the fader and put the two files out of phase, the vocal goes away. Nothing. That's what's supposed to happen. If you do that in Pro Tools, what you get is noise. Which means there are big-time phase problems. I've always kind of felt that way about Pro Tools; that it just kind of sounded like shit in general. I don't know why.

What's your studio setup like?

I'm using Apogee AD8000's. I like them because I like the big meters on all the inputs when I'm tracking. I'm going from there into an RME card into Nuendo and back out to a Neve summing box, the 8816. As far as monitoring, when I'm tracking I don't use Cubase. That's the other reason I have the AD8000's. I have the analog outs on all of them plugged into a monitoring desk so that I can just monitor the inputs when I'm tracking without dealing with any latency. Then, when I'm done tracking I bring everything into Cubase for editing and mixing.

What are some of the features in Cubase you use regularly?

I would say that the best thing I like about it is the Lanes feature, and the grouping of lanes for editing and comping drums and vocals. That works really well.

And the other thing that I really like about Cubase is that I can open more than one project at a time. I can go back and get stuff from other projects and just drag it. I can't have more than one project active at once, but I can still open up a project from three months ago and drag in that Dobro part I liked so much. I just drag it in and it not only comes in, but it comes in with all the automation associated with that track, all the EQs and plug-ins. That feature blows the minds of any engineers that come in here.

We recently brought in Kevin Killen as a consultant mixer on this Roseanne Cash record we just finished up. So I spent a week and a half with him tweaking mixes and stuff, and half the time we were working he was going, "Wow!" And he's been a longtime Pro Tools guy.

Do you mix in the box or with outboard gear?

It's a combination. I have a bunch of gear, old and new. I'm using the CC121 controller by Steinberg with the fader. I love that. It's so much better to do vocal rides or whatever when you have a fader. And, like I said, the analog outs are going into a Neve 8816 summing mixer. I have a patchbay where I can patch in all my outboard stuff as well.

Do you have any techniques that you've developed over the years that help you in your work?

I like that I can have my own mix set up with VST connections. I can have my kick, snare, bass, and lead vocal on separate mono outputs, have them labeled and save them as a template. Generally, I work with everything out the stereo output. I work fast and don't like to assign a bunch of different outputs. Then, when I mix, I bus everything out, because I want to use the panning and the analog summing of the Neve summing mixer. I haven't been totally convinced that summing in the box, in any of these things, is all that great. Plus, I want to use my compressor and print back to a MasterLink or back into the box. Any time I've done exports with a lot of math going on, meaning tons of automation and plug-ins and stuff, and then I do a mix and print it back into the box, I'm very consistently picking the mix that's printed back. I can't tell the difference when there is low math involved, if it's just a stereo track with no plug-ins or stuff and I export it. Then take that same track and print it back, then I can't really tell the difference. The summing debate has gone on a long time, even between different DAWs, as they have different audio engines.

What part of Cubase do you find the most helpful for mixing?

I use a lot of the effects. As a matter of fact, I've pulled in a lot of my Nuendo 2 plug-ins into Cubase 4. I had [Steinberg's] Greg Ondo up here, and I told him I liked a lot of the Nuendo 2 plug-ins, and he showed me how to put them into Cubase. So I pulled in all my favorite plug-ins from Nuendo, which makes me very happy.

I think the Reverb A is something they got completely right. The Multiband Compressor is awesome, on drums particularly. So I use some of those and a bunch of the new ones.

Any improvements you'd like to see in Cubase?

I said I love working in Lanes and doing comps and stuff. But let's say you've got 10 tracks of drums and you've done 10 passes. And each time you've done a pass you've grouped them, so you can switch back and forth between takes. Well, if I dump a take, or dump a couple of takes, I can't pull them higher up the lanes. In other words, when you expand the box to look at a bunch of takes, it will only expand so far, and after so many takes the waveforms will start going away. There's only so much space there. I would like to be able to expand the box infinitely, or at least be able to grab a file that is grouped to 10 other tracks, and pull it back up in the lane hierarchy where the spaces are, without ungrouping them and pulling them one by one.

Once you start dumping takes and you get down to the first take and the last take, you've now got seven takes of blank space there. You have to ungroup all of them and move each file individually up in the hierarchy and then regroup them. That's a major pain in the ass!

Cubase in Songwriting

For years, Steinberg used the tagline "Creativity First" to promote the idea that Cubase was much more than a computerized tape machine. The fact that Cubase has its roots in MIDI, where programming was seen as part of the creative process, and added linear audio recording later, has sustained it as a music creation platform.

From early on, Cubase was meant to be a complete system where you could take a musical idea and develop it, record it, arrange it, edit it, and mix it all in one place. Because of this, Cubase has been, and continues to be, an invaluable tool for songwriters and producers, from hobbyists to Grammy Award winners. In this chapter we'll hear from two such songwriter/producers, both longtime Cubase users, and how they have come to rely on Cubase over their years of doing high-level professional work.

VINCE MELAMED—SONGWRITER
Nashville, TN

Vince Melamed is an award-winning songwriter and keyboardist who has written for and performed with some of the biggest artists in the music industry. He has written or co-written songs for Trisha Yearwood, Phil Vassar, Cher, Tina Turner, and the Nitty Gritty Dirt Band, and has played and toured with Bob Dylan, the Eagles, Rosanne Cash, and Jimmy Buffett.

Tell me about the work that you do.

Well, I'm always songwriting, but I just released a solo album last week, which was the first I've ever done. I did it in a studio with a full band, and I used Cubase because I wanted to track it and get a real live feeling. At home I'm always layering one track on another, but I wanted to go in with a live band. I knew that if I played and sang at the same time I'd probably have to go back in and redo the vocal and the keyboard. So, what they [did was] give me rough mixes and I'd drop it into Cubase and do my keyboard parts and then send it back to the studio.

I also recently used Cubase for a competition for this Hillary Duff animated movie called *Food Fight*, which is yet to come out. There was this song available for the end title, and it was open to whoever thought they could do a good job. So we did it all in Cubase, and we got the gig.

Mainly I use Cubase for doing publishing demos. A lot of times I don't necessarily want to go into the studio, because in Nashville it costs about $800 to do a demo. And sometimes you can get a more raw feeling doing it right away, especially right after you've written the song. I may drop a few loops in, and hopefully the co-writer plays guitar, or we'll do vocals and all of it. And I've had some success; I think two or three major cuts. This Phil Vassar hit that I had ("I'll Take That as a Yes") was taken from a Cubase demo. And in that case it was probably better that it was done at home, because we just did it kind of funky. John McElroy, who is the co-writer, is a great guitarist, so just having him without the pressure of the studio, just hanging out and me playing the loop and whirly and John playing guitar — the demo just had a special personality. Somehow it got to Phil Vassar, and he really liked it and cut it. I think in that case had we gone in the studio and done a polished demo, it would have just been another song to him.

So, working with Cubase at home there was no pressure of the studio clock.

Exactly. And the funny thing was, it's kind of an R&B groove, and I put in a little banjo part on it just for fun, and they ended up using it on the record!

What version of Cubase are you using?

I'm using Cubase 5. Although I'm not fully taking advantage of all the new stuff yet; I just don't have the time. Some guys like to sit for days and days learning the new stuff, but I'm usually stacked up with demos or other stuff to do. I'll get to it, usually in a panic when I need something in there!

When did you first start using Cubase?

Oh, I think in 1994, when it was called Cubase Compact and it came on a floppy disk. I came to it from ADATs. But remember that during that time Cubase was still just a MIDI sequencing tool. [Steinberg's] Greg Ondo would come to the music stores in Nashville and give talks and demos, and he and I became friends. He asked me to try Cubase; I think it was 3.1 or the first version that did audio. He wanted me to try audio on it, and it took a while. We both had to grow as far as the PC catching up to the software's ability. [Alesis] ADATs [were] what everyone was using for audio at the time, but after I went over I never [went] back.

Can you tell me about your writing studio?

Sure. I've got an added wing on this house, and there's a room, or writing area, that's about 15 by 20 feet, which is great. Everyone can spread out, and we write the songs. Then we go into a much smaller room where I've got my studio set up. It's kind of neat because I can just hunker down in this little area and close the door and have all the wires be out of view from the rest of the house.

How about the equipment?

For hardware I've got the RME Hammerfall HDSP 9632, and I just use a Behringer ADAT interface with it, so I can have eight [inputs] and eight [outputs]. And I use lots of software instruments. For writing, a lot of times I will open Steinberg's Virtual Guitarist just to get into a groove. I'm a keyboard player, and I don't want to write piano songs. So I'll do anything, whether it's using a software instrument called Real Guitar, or [using] guitar samples from Native Instruments' Kontakt, so that it's not a piano. It just takes me somewhere else. Sometimes I'll use

Virtual Guitarist and just listen to it. It has some great rhythmic guitar playing, both acoustic and electric. And you can even take the acoustic guitar and add amp effects to it so it sounds like an electric. I also use DrumCore by Submersible Music.

Any outboard gear?

I don't use a lot of hardware anymore, and that's thanks to Cubase and the Universal Audio UAD card. But my basic mic pre — and all this stuff is like medium-grade — is a PreSonus Eureka that has been hot-rodded. And that's about it. Sometimes I'll use IK Multimedia's T-Racks at the end to run the mix through. And sometimes just for fun I'll run it through a Behringer Ultrafex. It's kind of like a poor man's [TC Electronic] Finalizer. So, you never know, just as long as you don't hold yourself to any rules or laws. Sometimes it comes out great, and sometimes it stinks.

For my keyboard controller, I still use a Roland Fantom. I will occasionally feed sounds from the Fantom via S/PDIF. And I have a little FaderPort by PreSonus to get around in Cubase.

When you start a song in Cubase, where do you start, and what's the process?

To be honest, I start basically with guitar, but when I really start writing from scratch, I use Ableton Live. I know it was originally supposed to be for DJs, but there's something about how you can drop in stuff and record tracks real fast and do verse, chorus, and so on. So I still use Live if I'm by myself trying to write from scratch.

Yesterday, there was an English band here from the '80s called Wet Wet Wet, kind of poppy MTV darlings, and I did some writing for them. I guess they're going to do another album. I used Live because I had to make a track really fast and present it to them so they could decide to write a song around it. So, today, I have the little work tape that was just recorded off a little handheld recorder, and I'm going to create a demo using Cubase. And when they go back to England, we'll send files back and forth. They are on Pro Tools, but it doesn't matter. We just export the files.

So, speed is really the key when you begin the writing process.

Exactly. I don't want to get bogged down by technical things. I use Ableton Live, where I've got all my software instruments set up on different channels and a microphone that I can sing into. I can present it quickly, and then come back and do the full demo in Cubase.

What are some of your go-to features in Cubase?

I'm a big fan of stack recording, especially when we have a vocalist come in. I have to say that the stack recording in Cubase is wonderful. I'll punch in something, and it creates a new track, and when we play it back, most of the time I don't even have to do any kind of peeling or anything. It's seamless; you don't hear any pops or clicks. There are a lot of great vocalists here in Nashville, but sometimes they don't have the patience to fix a line, or this and that. So stack recording mode is great. I just have to remember from the first take to put it in stack recording mode and set it properly. Then it's just a breeze; you've got maybe four or five different takes on a line that you can go back to.

And when you're mixing a demo, it's all within Cubase?

Yes. I mix within Cubase and then run the mix through Steinberg's WaveLab. That's where I might just do a little touch-up or something. I've had to tweak my mixes here and there. I'll play it somewhere and there's not enough of this or that, or the co-writer will come back and want me to change something.

Sounds like you do a lot of collaboration. Are you usually together or working over distance?

I do both. If a guy is in town for a while, then we'll write together. Of course, there are a lot of writers who live in Nashville. I have a friend in L.A. who will put guitar parts on some of my things, and I'll put keyboard parts on some of his things. It's so great now that I can give him a keyboard track and it always syncs. It really helps.

Most of my friends are on different platforms. There are still a lot of DP [Digital Performer] people, believe it or not, and a lot of Pro Tools [users]. So I just send WAV files or AIFF files. As long as we agree on what the tempo was and start it at measure one, it's no problem. I'll usually send them on a file-sending service.

What helps you the most for songwriting with Cubase?

The fact that I don't have to think about how to use it or do something with it. The thing is so intuitive, and it works. It does what it's supposed to do.

Any wishes for new features?

If I had a wish I'd love to see stack recording on MIDI. I guess they don't think that people want to do that, so what I have to do is route the MIDI from a software instrument to an audio track and use stack recording as an audio track.

JOCHEM VAN DER SAAG— PRODUCER, COMPOSER, ENGINEER
Los Angeles, CA

Jochem van der Saag is a versatile musician and programmer who works alongside legendary producer David Foster. He has been credited on numerous albums as a producer, co-producer, arranger, and engineer as well as a performer. With Foster, he has worked with such high-profile artists as Whitney Houston, Seal, Andrea Bocelli, Josh Groban, and Celine Dion.

What version of Cubase are you using?

Over the last two weeks I've finally had a little bit of a break in my schedule, so I upgraded to Cubase 5. I've had it running for quite a while, but I'm now officially doing my first album in Cubase 5, which is Andrea Bocelli.

What kind of work do you do?

For the last seven years I've been working with David Foster. For the last four or five years that's been pretty much exclusive, and over the last two or three years I've also gotten to a position where I co-produce with him on some projects and mix most of the records now. I'm freelance, but he's my number-one client, and takes up 95 percent of my time.

And David's role is mainly producing?

Songwriting, producing, and arranging. In my opinion, he's one of the best, maybe *the* best, pop arrangers in the business. How he works is he sketches out demos — his arrangements — to a level of very fine detail with virtual orchestration. What used to happen is he would give that to me, and I would add programming on top of it in terms of drums or keyboards or synths. Then he would give the strings to the string arranger, and work with that, and so on and so forth.

Do you work in your own studio?

For the last three or four years, he's asked me to come and set up at his studio. So now I have my own studio, which consists of two custom-built PCAudioLabs computers, and an identical setup over at his studio in Santa Monica. The systems have identical hardware and software, so that enables me to work with him over there, save the session on a external drive, take it home, and the session loads up exactly the same way as when we left off. Then I can work on it at my place, and when I take it back, the session comes up flawlessly. It's a great way of working because I can keep everything open and not have to print stuff to go from one place to the other.

When we start a song, we have to come up with a demo. We get a key, we get a tempo, and then I give him a click. He'll ask me for a piano sound or a guitar sound, and we start building it from there. That's all done in Cubase.

To make it possible for him to use all the latest virtual instruments at a low latency, I have two machines. Both of them have Cubase on them, and the first one is my master machine, where we build the session, record the MIDI, and record the audio. The second computer is basically a virtual synth machine that has Cubase loaded up with different templates — a classical template, a jazz template, a pop template, and so on. The two computers are then connected through MIDI over LAN, which gives me plenty of MIDI channels over a LAN cable. At the end of the day, all I have to do is save the presets from the synth machine over to the main machine, load up the plug-ins there, and then I've got it all in one session.

What hardware do the systems use?

It's all powered by RME hardware—the Hammerfall series PCI cards. I also have the [RME] Fireface that I used to use, but I discovered that the PCI card is just a little bit spiffier on the latency. Steinberg used to OEM the RME cards, and I use a couple of those as well.

You mentioned using VSTi's in the songwriting process. What are you using?

It varies from style to style. Earlier this year we did a Michael Bublé record, which is big-band jazz type stuff, and more recently we did a Katherine Jenkins record, which is more on the classical side. For strings I use various libraries loaded into [Native Instruments] Kontakt. The main samplers that I use are [Steinberg] HALion, Kontakt, and [Tascam] GVI, which gives me access to certain GigaSampler libraries that are either not available or don't translate well through HALion or Kontakt.

I'm a junkie when it comes to VSTi's. I own most of the stuff that's out there. All four of my machines have all of them on there, so the drag about that is, especially anything that uses Synchrosoft or iLok protection, I have to buy four versions of the same thing. It can get pretty pricey sometimes! The alternative is to carry dongles back and forth, but I'd rather be safe than sorry. I don't want to forget my dongle and then tell the artist that we can't open up the session!

In the songwriting process, how much is done virtually versus live?

When we're sketching it out, everything is done virtually. After that, we'll go into overdub land and record real piano, live orchestra, and vocals. It depends on the schedule of the vocalist when the vocals are recorded. Oftentimes we'll work with demo vocalists first if the singer is not available right away, or just to save them the time, and [they can] come in later and sing to a track that's more grown up, if you will.

Where do you record the live elements?

It depends on the size of the recording session. Vocals are always recorded at David's studio, which is very convenient, and most artists love it. With orchestras, it depends. For example, they just went to London and recorded the London Symphony Orchestra for the Bocelli project. The project we did before that with Katherine Jenkins, which was also a full-blown orchestra, we did at 20th Century Fox here in L.A. Sometimes we go to the Sony scoring stage as well. For rhythm section, tomorrow we're going to the Village Recorder, but for Bublé we did everything at Capitol Records. Really, anything outside of vocals we go to another studio to record.

How long have you been using Cubase?

I think about 23 years. Since the very beginning, when it was on the Atari. First it was only an Atari 1040ST with a floppy drive to save to. What I did before that was use two commercial cassette decks and a DJ mixer. I had one synth and one drum computer at the very beginning, and I would play a take and record it on one cassette deck. I would then play that back through the mixer and overdub another part to the other cassette deck. I would go back and forth so that at the end you ended up with one big chunk of hiss and a little bit of music! So I was happy when the Atari came around and MIDI was multitrack. Then I figured out that through FSK you could hang a little Tascam Portastudio 4-track on that. So, I did that until Cubase came out with audio.

People often ask me why I'm not on Mac or on Pro Tools, and I don't fight those wars anymore because I believe the best tool is the one that you make the best music with. But one thing that Digidesign will have to do is rewrite their code, because it still stems from the late '80s or early '90s, and it still has, at its core, the mono track implementation, a limitation of voices, and all these things.

To give you an example, this Bocelli project is in 96 kHz, and it goes to Abbey Road with about 40 tracks of stems prerecorded to overdub a full-blown orchestra, which is 25 or more mics with various room mics and all the close mics. Then, oftentimes we'll want to split up the sections and do strings with their room mics, and then brass, horns, and so forth. So it adds up to quite a bit, and one Pro Tools system can only do 96 tracks at 96 kHz. But Pro Tools uses one voice for playback and one voice for what it's going to record, so we wind up effectively with 48 tracks, which is not nearly enough. To get around that we have to slave two Pro Tools systems together—one for playback and one for recording. That gives you an example of how outdated the code is. I know Cubase will max out at like 500 tracks, but that's virtually unlimited for most purposes.

What feature or features do you find most important in Cubase?

One of the things I learned early on is that key commands are the way to take the technical part out of the way of creativity. The more keyboard shortcuts that are ingrained in your brain, the more speed you will have. The less you have to think about technically, the more you can think about what you want to do creatively. That's one of the most important things for me in working with Cubase.

Another thing I use all the time are the folder tracks. We are usually going to Pro Tools in the outside studios, not because we prefer it, but because that's what they have, and I always have to print stems of the tracks that we're currently working on. The folder tracks come in handy because I can stick a bunch of things in a folder, like sometimes I have crazy drum layering where I have eight different tracks that make up one sound. I can just stick all those in one folder track, and it helps keep my session clean and [lets me] easily create a stem. I use a program called MEAP (Multi Export Audio Pro), which is a Windows script written for Cubase that you tell how many tracks you want to print and where to put it and it exports it. The new Batch Export feature in Cubase is great, but the one thing that's missing from it that MEAP covers for me is the ability to organize it in folder tracks, solo them, and export them one at a time. I used to have to solo whatever folder track I wanted to export, type a file name, and then wait for three or four minutes and do this one at a time. MEAP does that all for me automatically.

How does Cubase help in the creative process?

One thing I use a lot in Cubase is templates. I'll take the time to make templates for different styles of music because it saves me so much time in the future. I'll load up whatever virtual instruments, routing, and master bus stuff that's appropriate for that style. If you're going to do an R&B track, you might want some hefty compression on your master bus and some top-end, [Spectrasonics] Stylus RMS, and some hip-hop or urban-type samples loaded into Kontakt or HALion, and it's ready to go. If you've got that organized, you can start working within a matter of seconds when inspiration strikes.

Another thing goes back to the unlimited track count. I do pretty detailed stuff sometimes when it comes to sound design, especially on the more orchestral albums, which tend to be almost cinematic. It's a lot of tracks with little shadow effects on them. Every little chunk of sound can have its own EQ and plug-in inserts, and so on.

I also use Warp mode a lot, especially in orchestral arrangements. David may play a rubato piece, and Warp is very helpful in clicking it out. It's not a static beat at all, but played completely free, and with Warp you can build a grid for it. It's extremely helpful for several reasons: one is you can then have a click, which you have to have if you want an orchestra to play to it; another is in terms of programming you now have a grid for a rubato piece of music, and you can quantize to something that's completely free-form.

One new thing that I've started using a lot is the VariAudio feature. I actually just used it on a mix we just finalized. I like it to add background vocals and pitch around delays. There are some things that I used to use Melodyne for, like audio-to-MIDI conversion, that is now right in the program. I have a lot of respect for the programming side of that, because VariAudio actually follows the editing very well. I think they implemented it very well.

How does Cubase help when you're working with vocalists?

David is known for being one of the best vocal producers in the business, and he does a lot with vocal comping. This year alone we had Seal, Michael Bublé, Whitney Houston, Natalie Cole, and Andrea Bocelli record right into Cubase. He loves working with me, and part of that are certain features when it comes to editing. The three different gain stages are very helpful in this. You have your regular fader automation, which every program has, then you have the gain level where you have a bunch of audio files that are grouped, and the third one is drawing automation in the waveform, which makes it very easy for other things like manually de-essing a vocal. Also, for vocal comping and not having to open up a fade editor when you want to do a fade, or shifting audio around while keeping your region edges exactly the same. All that stuff makes it easy.

Do you mix in Cubase?

One of the things that surprises people when I tell them is that I've mixed several albums in Cubase, all inside the box. I co-produced and mixed an album for Seal, which sold 2.7 million copies, and it was all done in Cubase. I was getting compliments from pros that have been in the industry a long time, and they were asking what console I mixed it on!

I tried to get into controllers, and I had a couple of Mackie controllers and I have a Frontier AlphaTrack, but I never touch them. I'm so used to mixing with the mouse that I really don't use them anymore. There are certain advantages to mixing with the mouse just because you can make changes not only at the point that you hear it, but also at other points in the track. For example, when I have to ride a vocal, I just start out doing basically a macro run of it to hear it, and after that I can adjust loud spots that I see on the screen. It's a little more efficient than just being locked into the moment that you hear it. I'm just so used to it that it works best for me.

From a historical perspective, what do you think is the biggest achievement in Cubase?

To me, the biggest, wisest, and most bold thing Steinberg did was to rewrite the code from scratch with Cubase SX. They had a blank sheet to write the technology that was taking leaps at the time. I think it was very bold, and it takes a lot of money and time. It's very easy to stay with the same thing and try to make that better. I think their audio engine is superior to anything else out there, and the fresh code made everything faster.

To give you a comparison, last year David did a big show called David Foster and Friends, which turned into a PBS special and DVD called *Hit Men*. David Reitzas recorded everything and did the surround mix, while I did all the editing—chopping and adding programming to it—with David. Just to give you an idea of the magnitude of it, it was a four-hour show with video, and we ended up with 441 tracks. This was a huge session! So, David Reitzas was working in Pro Tools in parallel on the same session and couldn't get 441 tracks into it. He was in the other room, so we had an exact comparison, and his session was like, you hit the spacebar and go get a cup of coffee, and it would start playback when you came back. It's a good comparison, because it was an attempt to play the same audio, same length, same video file, and Cubase was just leaving Pro Tools in the dust.

If I had to point to anything, it would be that Steinberg had the balls to start new, keeping all the good features that it's become famous for, and rewrite the technical part of it to keep up with the technology that's out now.

Is there anything you think is missing from Cubase?

One thing, and this is just a dream of mine, but at some point in the future I would like to see spectral editing implemented at the multitrack level. Not just to fix things, but in addition to, or even to replace, EQ as an insert on a track. You see the frequency on the vertical axis, the timeline on the horizontal axis, and intensity of color indicates what energy you have at what time and frequency. Then having brushes or functions that you can edit on that and have complete spectral control over the track. For example, if the guitars sound a little bit harsh in just one bar, you can just take a paint brush and maybe soften them up a little bit. That would be awesome.

Cubase in Video Game Music

9

Music and sound for video games is an area that has exploded along with the popularity of the games themselves over the past several years. As graphics and story lines have gotten more intricate and elaborate, the music and sound effects in games have had to keep pace. This has spawned an entire arm of the audio production industry all its own.

In chapter 9, we'll go behind the scenes of one of the biggest video game franchises on the market and see how Cubase plays an integral part in the hectic pace of audio production for the medium.

JORIS DE MAN—
COMPOSER AND SOUND DESIGNER
West Sussex, UK

Joris de Man is a classically trained composer who has scored numerous film, TV, and video game projects. Beginning his musical training with the violin at the age of 6, he later became intrigued with synthesizers and computers and combined technology with his classical roots to carve out a unique musical identity. His powerful, epic composition style for orchestra and his skill in working with technology led him to become the audio director of Guerrilla Games/Sony's *Killzone* video game franchise.

Tell me about the kind of work that you do.

I'm a composer and sound designer, although in the past few years I've mainly been doing compositional work. I write music for video games, and the last big game that I worked on was *Killzone 2* for the PlayStation 3. I've basically been working on that franchise for the past few years. Even though it's called *Killzone 2*, it's the first game in the franchise. There have been two other games, one for the PlayStation 2 and one for the PlayStation Portable.

My main focus is writing music for that game, which comes in two different flavors. One is the "in-game" music you hear while you're playing the game, which is usually done using MIDI and samples and software instruments. And the other is the music for what they call the "cut scenes," which are basically the little movies that you see in between playing the game that advance the story line and tell you about what's happening in the game and what's happening to the character; giving you a bit of background as to what you're doing and why you're doing it. Those bits we tend to do with live orchestra.

On the last game we recorded a full symphony orchestra. I think we had between 70 and 80 players, and we recorded it at Abbey Road Studios in London. My task was to get those bits together and deliver them; some of which was done in 5.1 surround, so we used Nuendo for that, and the other music was done in stereo, or "fake surround," so to speak. When Cubase 5 came out, there were so many cool features that I thought it would be excellent for music composition and production, and I wanted to get in there early.

How did you start using Cubase?

I used to be a die-hard Logic Mac fan and running Pro Tools concurrently with that, and I thought it was the best thing in the world. Which was fine; it kind of served me until I did the first *Killzone*, which was a really heavy MIDI arrangement. For all the music that I do, I need to do really detailed MIDI mock-ups, use a copyist, and then take them to the scoring stage and record them live. In film instances, especially with games, some of those MIDI mock-ups tend to remain in the MIDI stage and just need to sound really realistic. Once we recorded the orchestra stuff and I had to actually mix it, I found that just doing quick edits like crossfades across 24 tracks of the microphone positions in the orchestral recording took absolutely too long. You would do one cut and the machine would be calculating crossfades, and after three or four cuts it was ridiculous. [I thought] "There has to be a faster way of doing this."

At that point I went to my local music shop, and they had Nuendo, and I had a quick look at it. I had read about it, and around that time Nuendo 2 was announced, and I thought it could be pretty good. So, they showed me the real-time crossfades, and I thought, "Wow, this is it!" And I wasn't even really seeing it as a MIDI alternative; I was mainly looking at it in terms of audio editing. Also, at the end of the first *Killzone* project, I was running really heavy Logic sessions with the EX24 sampler; like 62 instances of that. And it didn't really deal very well with the heavy load. I used to get things like hanging notes and notes playing that weren't even supposed to be playing at that point. It was just getting really messy. So messy that I couldn't even do a proper export for my copyist to listen to what it's supposed to sound like.

To cut a long story short, I decided that the whole Mac thing wasn't really working for me anymore. It was still Mac OS 9, and everything was going toward Mac OS X, but it was still very messy. So I decided to look at Nuendo; I knew that it could do great audio editing, but MIDI-wise it was looking pretty good as well. So I took the plunge, bought a big PC, and haven't really looked back. I've been using it and Cubase on everything since, and I'm really glad I did, because it's been a lot better in many respects.

Sounds like you work the MIDI and audio sides together.

That's correct, yeah. On an average session, if I'm doing a MIDI rendition I'll have about 160 MIDI tracks and probably another 20 to 30 audio tracks. Because of my sound design background, I do a lot of things in audio as opposed to MIDI. Like if I've got some heavy hits or percussive things, or some musical sound design, then I'll just use audio tracks for that. Or I'll create some sounds first in a separate session and bounce those out as audio files so I can manipulate them a little bit more and add them to the MIDI session.

MIDI-wise, it's pretty heavy as well, although I've heard of some people having something like 300 MIDI tracks. I'm not quite as bad as that. I usually have about 12 to 14 multitimbral VST instruments running at the same time, and three or four Kontakt instances. There's a new plug-in that I'm using for orchestra renditions that's really, really good. I don't think a lot of people are using yet, but it's by Wallander Instruments. It's quite interesting. It's mainly for brass and woodwinds, although [they're] looking at doing strings as well. And it's not sample-based or physical modeling, either. It's almost like some sort of additive synthesis. I think it uses a combination of additive synthesis and impulses. They use it to simulate live brass instruments. And it sounds absolutely amazing, and it reacts very realistically in terms of performance. It's also very light: one instance will only take up about 5 MB. So you can load up a bunch of instances and really get some realistic renditions.

I use GigaStudio in addition, with MIDI over LAN. I've got one additional computer running in the background to do that kind of stuff. I'd say 50 percent of all the samples and stuff that I'm running are actually on the main machine because it's a fast quad-core machine. I'm running Vista 64, which is somewhat unusual. I've not heard of many people doing it because they don't think it runs very well. I've actually had a very good experience with it. I run Cubase and Nuendo in 32-bit mode, but then use ReWire to go back into Cubase to get some more instances. It basically lets me run more instances without running out of memory. Once you reach the 3.2 GB limitation in 32-bit mode, it starts getting a bit hinkey. The benefit of ReWire is when you bounce stuff out. You can actually do an offline bounce and it will render correctly—most of the time anyway.

How is your studio set up?

I've got the PC, which runs Cubase and Nuendo. I'm using an RME Fireface 400 as my audio interface. I've got an old Pro Tools setup that I'm running on a separate machine. I'm not actually using Pro Tools itself, but just using it as a mixer because I want to keep everything digital. So, I've got three audio interfaces: an 882, a 1622, and an ADAT Bridge, and it literally act as a mixer. Once it goes in there, using an ADAT Lightpipe I can pipe things back into Cubase and Nuendo. I do the same thing with the GigaStudio PC, which is just an old Dell machine. That's got an RME Digi96 with simple ADAT in and out. And that also pipes into Pro Tools. Then I can apply some reverb with an old LexiVerb plug-in on there, which is actually very decent. I've got a Lucid GENx clock to clock all the digital audio interfaces together. It's just one master clock that manages everything. That makes it very easy.

I also have a bunch of hardware synths: a Roland XV-5080 for bread-and-butter sounds, an E-mu Morpheus for some additional sounds, a Waldorf Microwave, and an E-mu E4K as a master keyboard. But so much of it these days happens internally. I use Kontakt 2 and 3 a lot, Absynth, a bit of Reaktor, Omnisphere, Stylus RMX, and quite a lot of custom sound design.

How about sample libraries?

Yes, obviously I use a whole bucket load of libraries. I've got a little bit of VSL (Vienna Symphonic Library) before they started doing their own instruments. I think I've got Opus, or — I don't even remember what it's called now! I think I've got some Sonic Implants and some Quantum Leap Orchestral Percussion as well.

Personally, I find that not using one particular library in its entirety kind of allows me to create a more interesting and more unique sound. I might use percussion from one library and some strings from another library. I really like the violins from VSL, but I'm not a huge fan of their lower strings like the double bass and the celli. So, I might use Sonic Implants for that. I've also done some custom programming in Kontakt to get the kind of sounds that I want and have them behave the way I want, and so they don't sound like the libraries everyone else is using. Once you start piling things up, it can become unmanageable. It's harder to separate in the mix. It's really a matter of finding what works, really. Sometimes I just find one string patch may work better than another or for the density of the arrangement. I think custom programming is a great way to go.

Do you incorporate live tracks into your projects?

I don't do live tracks very much because it's either that they want everything in MIDI with no budget to add anything to it, or it's all done live. What I've done in the past, which has worked quite well, is reuse some leftover tracks from earlier projects. For example, on the first *Killzone* we recorded this solo vocalist, and then on the second game, I did everything with MIDI. I was able to re-edit the solo vocalist that I got on the first game and overlay it with the MIDI stuff. I found that it added a tremendous amount of feeling to it because there's this live element over it.

I've done a few bits of live recording here in my studio, but it's not really well equipped to work with live musicians. I play a little bit of violin, and I overdubbed some live electric violin on one of the pieces, and I had an old beaten-up guitar that I retuned one of the strings and then used it as a really bad-sounding bass guitar. That was the idea, that it had to sound really broken. So, I've done some stuff like that, but my space is really a writing studio, and when I need to record stuff live I usually go to another studio.

Do you use the scoring features of Cubase?

I've used them a little bit. I was very interested in XML, in being able to export an XML file. That was quite useful. But I've found in practice, especially with the time consideration, that to set up all the tracks and export everything to XML took too long, and for the copyist it was easier just to have a MIDI file. I have to reorganize everything anyway and merge a lot of tracks together, so the XML feature is not that useful for me. I'll just import the MIDI tracks into Sibelius, which is what my copyist uses.

Also, I don't really work much with key switches. If I have different articulations in performance, like staccato or legato, I do them on separate tracks. It makes your template a little bit bigger, but it's much quicker and easier to see what a particular instrument is doing at any time. So, if someone comes back to me and says that in bar 5 or bar 6 that instrument is supposed to be playing tremolo, then it's much easier to go back into my session and see it.

I'm very interested in VST Expression in Cubase 5, because I think that could change things. Then, you could see the articulations in the score editor and could work in the same way. But I've not yet had a chance to convert my templates to start using it. It will mean that with custom libraries, I'll need to start using key switches to program it all in. That's the downside, really; that if you're using custom libraries, you'll have to do a bit of setup on the Expression Maps to build it all in. It's something I want to explore a bit more.

How do you organize large sessions?

I've got a few different templates. What I tend to do as I go along in a project is save different versions of the song that I'm working on as a template so that I have a big orchestral template that I can use if I have to start a new session. I've always found that a very useful feature. The only downside is that you need to delete all your files from the session. Even though it's called a template, it's really a reference to a regular project file. So, if there's audio or MIDI tracks in there, it will literally just load that session. I think they should make it that if you save it as a template, it's just empty, and just keeps the instruments and so on of your session.

My templates tend to develop a little bit during the project. At the start of a project I might spend some time setting this whole thing up and just make sure I've got all areas covered. And then, once I've composed two or three pieces, I'll find that that string patch or that brass patch or whatever is not working, or that I need another few tracks for this or that. And so my template expands a little bit, and I'll save a new version of it. It's a very good way to start a new piece.

Are there any features or techniques you rely on for video game work?

There are a number of things that I've found very useful. One is folder tracks. I've found that they really help me in terms of editing and moving things around, which tends to happen a lot when you're editing to picture or doing music for in-game pieces. The producers will come back to you and say it's great, but they need another few bars at the beginning, or this needs to be extended a little bit.

Just to give you an overview of what my sessions look like, I'll split the Project window in two so that on the top I've got an extra timeline under the toolbar. So I know how long everything is, and I add a marker track to mark things out, and an arranger track. The arranger track is very important for in-game music, especially if you're writing interactive music. It's a real time-saver. I have to make sure that pieces of music can fit to other pieces, so I'm almost composing in a pattern-based way. The arranger track is really good in that sense because you can mark things out and quickly try out different ideas with a different order of patterns. That was really instrumental in doing the instrumental music for *Killzone 2*. I would just mark all those bits out and listen to them in separation to make sure that they worked randomly.

So, that's at the top of the Project window, and of course I have the audio and MIDI tracks underneath. And everything is in folder tracks. I have one folder track that encapsulates everything. In that "All" folder track there will be a folder for MIDI and a folder for audio. Then, inside the MIDI folder each instrument section — brass, strings, percussion, choir — will have its own folder track again. Then I may even separate it further. This is really great because if you need to move anything around, you can just cut, copy, and paste in the "All" folder track and the whole session, everything underneath it, will move with it. I find this is a much easier way to do it than to use the Range Edit and Global Copy or Insert Time or Delete Time. The only thing that won't move with it, and it's a bit annoying, is the time and signature track, but that's easy enough to move around on its own.

So, it sounds like there are many changes and adjustments during a project.

Yeah. And I have to be flexible. I suppose it's similar when you're scoring a film. If you're scoring a "cut scene," as they call it in game speak, they often come back and say they've changed the scene. A lot of the cut scenes will take place in a game environment, and so if the game environment changes because a level designer finds a section of the game doesn't play very well, they change it or change the setting. Then, that affects the people who have actually directed and made those cut scenes, and so they'll have to create a new version that takes into account the changes from the level designers. This often changes the timing of the music as well.

Where do you (the music) come into the production process of a game?

It's usually around the midpoint, because they also have to figure out exactly how they're going to do the music. They have to have an engine that plays back the music, especially when the game has interactive music. There is usually a bit of time required sitting with the game designers and figuring out how the interactive music is actually going to work. How does it react to what the players are doing? What changes are important and what changes aren't important?

On *Killzone 2*, because it's a first-person shooter and there is a lot of running and gunning, the music has to be interactive, but the interactivity can be pretty black and white. It's either all-out action and shooting, or it's sneaking around. There's really not that much in between. So, the types of music that we needed to have were either quite subtle eerie ambiance exploration music or very percussive and very aggressive action music with some transitions between those.

With sudden shifts in action, how do you deal with the musical transitions?

Again, this is where the arranger track in Cubase really comes into play. One of the problems that we had was there was an issue when you switch from a high-intensity piece to a low-intensity piece of music. When you have an 8-bar segment that is very intense and another that is not very intense, and you piece those two together, you're going to hear a hard cut. So, one of the ways we solve that is by using release tails. We would have two bars of reverb and audio dying out from that previous section and it would be mixed together with the lower-intensity music.

That's a technique that we used on *Killzone 2*, and it was really easy to do with the arranger track. Because it was still MIDI, I could just create an empty 2-bar pattern and insert it between every other pattern. So, I could have 8 bars of music and 2 bars of emptiness, another 8 bars of music and 2 bars of emptiness, and so on. Once the MIDI stopped playing, the live reverb I used in the session would capture the decay of the sounds dying out. Being able to use the arranger track in that way and quickly move things around without messing up the session was absolutely invaluable.

Any custom techniques that you've come up with on your own?

One of the things I would highly recommend to anyone is [PI Engineering's] X-keys keypad. You can use it to create shortcuts for all the keys. The other things it can trigger are macros, and macros are something that I've gotten heavily into. I've got macros for exporting selected tracks or something that's soloed. One of the things I tend to do when I'm editing a large piece of audio is to make certain cuts and then move them down to a track below. I've created a macro for this that does it automatically. I've got a macro for renaming tracks, which I find very useful. I've created some macros for MIDI exporting; for example one that deletes all the muted MIDI parts and removes empty tracks so that once I give something to my copyist, I'm sure he doesn't get things that are not meant to be there.

This is a bit of a hack, but it's one of the things I've missed from Logic. If I'm copying something from one part to another part, I need to paste it at the origin so it's in the exact spot timing-wise. I made a macro that will basically create a marker point at the start position and then go to that marker when pasting. Nothing earth-shattering, but I've found macros to be big time-savers, especially when used in combination with X-keys. I don't have to remember anything, I just press the key on the X-key and it's done. It's sped up my workflow considerably.

One of my X-keys is for the MIDI side and one is for the audio side. On the MIDI side, I've got all the quantize values, things like select the same octave, select all, select invert, things for transposing so I can quickly transpose notes up and down. If I want to double a line I have a macro that takes a line, copies it, and transposes it an octave. I've got a macro that triggers a logical preset that randomizes the velocity or the position, if I'm trying to create some realism so it's not so rigid.

One of the things I often find is that controller keyboards sometimes create data that you don't necessarily want. For example, if you're playing hard or loud parts on your keyboard, you may find that you're triggering aftertouch when you don't really want to. And aftertouch sometimes triggers vibrato in certain samples, so you end up getting vibrato in places that you don't really want it. So, I created a quick Logic preset that just deletes all the controller data from a track or a MIDI part. I put that on the X-key as well.

I also have quick things like fixing the length of notes, because if the notes are too long on a percussion part and I'm quantizing it, then actually the length of the notes will go over the other notes. It may cause notes not to be triggered. I did a Logic preset that fixes notes to the quantize level that I've selected.

Is there something you'd like to see in Cubase that's missing?

One thing is being able to edit pitch-bend data as automation. I'm able to edit everything else as automation, especially with the new automation features in Cubase 5, where they're actually now connected. The MIDI control can drive the automation or the other way around. They're not hampering each other anymore. I think it's a fantastic feature because there used to be a discrepancy where if you recorded track automation data that modifies a MIDI parameter, and then you recorded a MIDI track that was also modifying the same MIDI data, you would get a big mess. The fact that you can now use one to trim the other is a huge time-saver. I just find it ridiculous that you can't do it with pitch-bend data! It doesn't show up in the controller list.

The other thing is multi-export, which is improved in Cubase 5. But you still can't export in the same way that you can with Multi Export Audio Pro (MEAP). It's a multi-export tool for Cubase and Nuendo and basically uses a script to export all the audio tracks. If you want to export like eight or nine VST MIDI tracks—it might be that they're even running from the same virtual instrument but you want them separately as stems—this tool will automate the process. It works pretty well. In Cubase 5, you can only render the one output from the VST instrument track.

Cubase in Live Music

10

Technology has become an integral ingredient in live music at every level, from a coffeehouse performer playing backing tracks from an iPod to a stadium tour running music, lights, and multimedia from banks of computers under the stage. At the highest level, DAWs are not only used to record songs, but also to perform them live, often with the same material from the studio. In this chapter we'll hear how Cubase is used in preproduction and live performance for some of the biggest stadium tours in recent years.

PAUL MIRKOVICH—
MUSICAL DIRECTOR,
KEYBOARDIST, COMPOSER
Los Angeles, CA

Whether in the studio, onstage, or on TV, Paul Mirkovich has been performing and recording for more than 20 years. After studying with Henry Mancini, Lalo Schifrin, and Claire Fischer at the Grove School of Music, Mirkovich went on to record with such artists as Peter Gabriel, Cher, Janet Jackson, and Shawn Colvin. He has performed on TV shows including *The Tonight Show*, *The Late Show with David Letterman*, *Saturday Night Live*, and *Good Morning America*. His experience in working with artists has led to a series of successes as musical director for both TV shows and live tours, most notably the CBS show *Rock Star: INXS*, *Cher: The Farewell Tour*, and Pink's Funhouse Tour.

You've used both Nuendo and Cubase. Which are you on now?

Setting up the current Pink tour, most of my work was done in Cubase 5. I tend to use whichever one is the latest version. So I used Nuendo 4 when that was out, and Cubase 4 before that. I find that the products are very similar. I actually really loved the interface of Nuendo 4. I thought it was really strong and clean. So when that came out I stopped using Cubase 4. Now I'm on Cubase 5 because it's a lot stronger in a lot of ways. There are still some things I liked about Nuendo 4 better, just from an interface standpoint, the way it looked and the way it acted. But I just like to learn the new stuff when it comes out.

When did you first start using Steinberg software?

I think it was 1990. I actually had Cubase on the Atari when it was first available. That was my first awareness of it, on the Atari 1040ST with built-in MIDI and all of that. Before it really did audio, it was just a MIDI sequencer.

What kind of work do you do with Cubase?

Besides putting live shows together, I do a lot of session work in L.A., where people will send me a stereo mix of a track and I'll pull it into Cubase, play all my stuff around it, and send it back. I do a lot of work for different jingle houses in L.A. as well, where I do tracks for anything from radio packages to TV shows and composing. There's a group of shows on ABC that I've done composing for: *Super Nanny*, *The Biggest Loser*, and stuff like that. I put all my tracks into this pool, and they use them on three or four shows on ABC. That's more straight composition. Then there are things like radio packages for European radio stations, where I'll do fifteen 20- to 30-second things in a week's time and then bring my tracks in and we'll record to them.

In addition to the live tours I've put together for Cher and Pink, I do a lot of other live work. I just did a TV show for MTV called *Star Maker* with Mark Burnett and P. Diddy. Besides all of the music prep that I do for the band, we play to tracks and clicks in Cubase. So, if it's a hip-hop or an R&B song and there are tracks that we're going to play along with, they'll run them from Cubase.

Tell me about your rig.

I have a studio at my house with three computers that run Cubase and various samplers. I have some Muse Receptors that I have linked up to Cubase as well, and everything kind of ports into my Mac Pro running Cubase 5.

You also use a lot of virtual instruments.

Yes. I'm way into it. I've been using the Receptors for years, and that's all they are: virtual instruments. They interface really well with Cubase 5 with an Ethernet connection. But, yeah, I use just about every virtual instrument you can possibly think of! I have all that and like 12 synthesizers sitting in my room too, so I use both. But most of the heavy sample stuff, especially the drum machine and loop stuff, is pretty much always inside Cubase.

How about sample libraries?

I have a Sonivox orchestra library that I like. I've got the Native Instruments Komplete 5. I've got all the Spectrasonics stuff, and then a couple more unusual ones like [reFX] Vanguard, which is a great one, and some of the [Nomad Factory] Blue Tubes stuff. It's pretty amazing, the amount of stuff out there. I'm probably leaving out most of the stuff I have. I really like the new drum machine in Cubase 5. It's really easy to use and sounds really good. I haven't really gotten into LoopMash yet; I don't really do that kind of thing. But the meat-and-potatoes drum machine, Groove Agent One, I like a lot. I just got the beta for the new Grand 3, by Steinberg. It's pretty stunning! I was very impressed with it. Really playable, and I'm looking forward to using it a lot more.

Is it a big challenge to keep track of all your instruments and sounds?

Well, the only problem is that sometimes you have too much stuff to pick from. The other part of it is, the drum stuff and the loop stuff are just to get you going on a track. You can always replace it. A lot of times I'll just throw something up that has a tempo that I like and play to it. Then I'll change the rhythm of the loop or change the loop itself if I don't feel it's exactly working with where the track goes. The great thing is I can call up Groove Agent One to get a basic beat down and replace it later. I don't do a lot of dance type music, so eventually someone's going to play real drums anyway. And I'm not one of those guys that likes to spend 12 hours making a drum track that I can have my friend, the drummer, play in three minutes and it's going to be superior to it. But at least I can get the idea across really well and leave the stuff that the drummer can't do, like a cool loop sound that's filters or certain effects, something that's a little more out-there.

Do you use MediaBay in Cubase?

MediaBay is confusing to me, to be honest with you. It's a little overwhelming at times, and at times I find it doesn't work like they say it's supposed to work. Maybe it's my limitation on how I'm trying to set it up or where I have everything put together, but simple things, like I click on a WAV file and it doesn't play in my song. Well, that's what it's supposed to do. If I find something I like in there, I just drag it in anyway. I'm organized in some ways, but in that way, no.

How about VST Expression?

I like the idea of it. Unfortunately, it doesn't work with my library as of yet, the Sonivox stuff. I'm interested to see how they're going to make that work. It certainly would make it a lot easier if I'm writing a string part and I can just go into the score and draw a slur and some staccato dots and something marcato and have it just play the right samples. That would be amazing. From my understanding, in order to make it work for third-party stuff, you would have to go through a process of setting it up manually, which would be pretty tedious. At this point it's just quicker for me to play the part in marcato if I want and then have another MIDI channel that has staccato or a control switch or whatever.

How do you use Cubase to set up a live tour?

When you set up a tour, a lot of it is organizational, in figuring out what tracks from the record are going to be played live and what's going to be played by the box. Then there are composition elements. If the artist wants to do something radically different on a song, then I have to pretty much recompose it, or if there are intros and endings that have to be done, or an overture, which there is a lot of times. In video pieces and dance breaks between songs, where the artist is off taking a breather or changing clothes or whatever, then I've got to compose a piece that fits or links songs together. Many times over video there's remixes of a lot of different material from a lot of different songs that have to be homogenized together. All the sounds in the show that are being played by the box have to be delivered to the front of house mix. Then the rest of the sounds being played by the musicians have to be programmed into their various rigs. Where it's desired, everything can sound exactly like the record, given the variance of live players and a live environment. Then, the stuff that you intentionally want to be different from the record has to sound just as powerful and just as good.

Also, a lot of times when I'm building a song, say for Pink, I have all the raw Pro Tools tracks from the record, but unfortunately I never get the tracks with any of their plug-ins. I just get the raw audio that was recorded, and nothing of what they did to it afterward. So, I basically have to recreate those sounds if they have specific delays, EQs, or compression. I have to recreate that because I'm not going to send the front of house engineer 65 tracks of stuff. I'm going to send him eight to 12 tracks that are submixed into drum loops, basses, guitars, any extra background vocals, any effects, and percussion. Anything that the live band is not playing has to be submixed into appropriate groups, and then I have to recreate the mix of those that were from the record so that when they are added to the live band, it reproduces the song.

In a tour like Cher or Pink, the music coming from the box is equally as important as the live band, because without it, it won't sound like the song on the record. And without the live band, it just sounds like some dead tracks.

What is the setup onstage?

I don't actually run Cubase live. We do all of the material ahead of time in rehearsal, and then when I have all the submixes I want, I bounce them down to just straight audio, and that plays out of computers running Digital Performer. Which is kind of the standard that most people have been using for that particular function for years, because it's very stable and really good at that aspect. There are some functions that DP has that are really good for being able to switch songs and audio on the fly. It has a chaining function, which has made it the standard for that. Some people use Pro Tools as well, but Pro Tools is a little iffy live.

Are other elements of the show locked with that as well—lighting, video, etc?

Oh, yeah. There are bands that are still just rock bands that just go out and play—four guys on a bare stage—but most shows nowadays use more. Even bands that you would consider heavy rock 'n' roll bands are linking all of their audio to their lighting and their video. Once you enter into the multimedia world in live performance, it all has to be synced or it doesn't make sense.

In the Pink show, we're all running off the same SMPTE code: audio, video, and lighting. When we're playing the song "So What," we can have the *So What* video playing in the background, and it's in perfect sync. Or, when she's doing "Ave Maria," which is another one of her songs, there's been video created specifically for that song and lighting effects that are very emotionally attached to the song. If they were out of sync, it wouldn't have the same impact. When you see it all together, it's pretty stunning.

How does Cubase help you compose new material for live shows?

That's another element of the live shows. There is a lot of composition that's involved in the whole thing. I'm creating stuff that makes the show seamless between songs, under video, remixing stuff. For the overture of the Cher show, I had a two-minute piece under video that had to encapsulate her entire 40-year career. I had a dance beat, but I also mixed in "I Got You

Babe" from the '60s and "Gypsies, Tramps, and Thieves," and all these different elements. The great thing about doing this in Cubase is I don't have to worry about what the format is. I don't have to worry about it being 16-bit or 24-bit anything. I just drag everything into one session and move it all around, which is something none of the other programs do. I don't understand why none of the others do that. You always have to convert it and it slows down your workflow when you have to wait for it to convert all the time.

I also have to tempo- and pitch-match stuff. If I want everything at 130 bpm, I have to take all these various elements that are quite a bit slower, some are in different keys, so I have to pitch- and time-correct stuff to match this tempo. It's really simple to do in Cubase 5. I just drag and drop and then drag the ends to whatever tempo I want it to be, change the pitch of it to whatever I want it to be, and it's pretty easy.

I did one thing for the Cher show that was really cool. She did a song called "The Beat Goes On," which she sang with Sonny many years ago. There was a video of the two of them singing it that was never really released, but it was a video from like 1966 or 1968 or something of the two of them singing this song. She wanted to be able to sing the song live with Sonny on video and not have her old vocal in there. So what I had to do was find two bars of the song where it's just the groove, and cut and paste that and copy it for the entire three-and-a-half-minute song, and then further cut and paste the bars where he sang, and put it in the appropriate places. Then I had to apply a high-pass filter so I didn't have the bottom end from that bar clouding the bottom end from the bar I just pasted. I had to take every bar and time-correct every beat, one beat at a time, so that it all matched, which was a huge endeavor.

Then, I had the issue of the bar of the groove and the bar with Sonny's singing coming over it and all of a sudden it gets louder because it was twice as much stuff happening. I had to create a horn section where I used the [Fable Sounds] Broadway Big Band horn library to create the horn parts. Then I had to get the band to play over the top of it and have it all work. So when people watch it they see her come out, and he's on the video singing, and she's singing live with him. It's pretty cool. I remember thinking when I was doing it in Cubase 5 that if it had been five years earlier, either there would have been no way to do it, or it would have taken me forever. I did it in about two or three hours!

Is everything timed to the second in a live show, or are there spaces for improvisation and other things?

In both the Pink show and the Cher show, not every song is played to the box. The majority of the songs are timed, but there are also a couple of songs where it starts out with the box and at the end it goes free-form, and then the box kicks back in at a later point. So, there are moments where it's more free and not completely rigid. But a lot of the stuff where there is lighting and video and dancers and all of that, it has to be the same way every night.

Are there changes to the set or arrangements during the course of a long tour?

Yeah. In fact, today I'm going in to work on two new songs that Pink wants to add for America, and three other songs that we haven't done in quite a while that she wants to do for a video shoot. So, it's kind of a busy time right now, and we're going to change up some stuff. Also, the artist will get tired of stuff and want to add or change things from time to time.

Do you have any favorite go-to features in Cubase?

Time correction and pitch correction I do all the time. I may do a whole track for something and need to change it. I don't usually pitch a whole track up or down, but I certainly change the tempo of things after they're done. When I'm composing, I like to group stuff. I like to mix in groups rather than mix individual tracks.

The virtual instruments have changed the entire way I do music. They are huge for me as a keyboard player. Not only can I save my mix, I can save all my instrument settings and set up a template with the whole thing. I open up Cubase, and immediately four or five of my favorite virtual instruments pop up on the correct channels with MIDI, EQ setups, and so on. It saves me 20 minutes of setting stuff up. It certainly has made things easier. The trap with having so many choices is to not get stuck looking through too many sounds without making a decision. So I like to start from the same place every time and it won't always end up in the same place, but hopefully someplace different.

Templates are brilliant. I have different templates set up depending on what I'm doing. If I'm doing a straight composing thing I'll bring up a more orchestral setup. If I'm doing a track where I know I'm going to be singing 16 vocal parts, I have a template that comes up with a drum machine, bass, and piano, and all the vocal channels ready to go. If you set up templates based on what you're doing that day, it saves a huge amount of time.

In doing so many tours and live TV, do you have any technology horror stories?

This isn't a live performance story, but it's one of my favorite Nuendo stories. Years ago, I was doing a Janet Jackson tour, and I was sitting with Jimmy Jam and Janet. This was right when Nuendo just came out. I was the first guy doing anything on Nuendo on the Mac. I was using a beta for the whole show and it had performed beautifully, and I was bragging about it, how great it was. So, I was doing some audio editing on some tracks for the show with Jimmy and Janet. We sat there for about two hours, and I was editing as we were talking about it, and it was all done. Everything was beautiful. Jimmy said, "OK, that's great. Let's put that in the show." And when I went to export all the audio, it erased the right side of every track in the piece. And I couldn't stop it! It was doing it right in front of me! I got to the end, and Jimmy just looked at me, and he said, "Well, you know what we did. Just do it again." So they left and I had to do it all over again from memory.

Cubase in Electronic Music

11

The very nature of recording music on a computer lends itself well to the creation of electronic music. From the earliest computer-based recording systems, electronic music producers have used every bit of new technology they could get their hands on to advance this popular genre. In the early days, using MIDI to control the burgeoning number of synthesizers on the market provided new ways to build intricate arrangements. Later, combining MIDI with audio loops, sound effects, and mixing techniques advanced recordings even further. Today, most music creation has moved inside the box to take advantage of the sea of available virtual instruments. From faithful recreations of the classics to eclectic specialty instruments and realistic sample libraries, there is a seemingly endless supply of tools at the disposal of electronic musicians.

KRAFTWERK

Formed in the early 1970s, the German band Kraftwerk is considered by many to be a pioneer in electronic music, both in the studio and in live performance. Ralf Hütter and Florian Schneider started experimenting in their own Kling Klang Studios with sound and video, from which came a series of influential albums and live performances. The group's early experimental sound quickly gave way to undulating rhythms and memorable melodies that were driven by early synthesizer and sequencer technology, and later polished and expanded with the advent of computer recording technology. In addition to sequenced tracks, Kraftwerk uses computers on stage as instruments, often improvising various parts of their shows against a multimedia backdrop.

Although the Kraftwerk lineup has included 11 members over the past four decades, founding member Hütter remains, along with Fritz Hilpert, Henning Schmitz, and Stefan Pfaffe.

Kraftwerk has been using computer technology since its beginnings. How long have you been using Cubase?

Fritz Hilpert: Kraftwerk started using Cubase during its early version, when it was called Cubeat and ran on the Atari ST. In the late 1980s we redesigned Kling Klang Studios to be completely digital. We used Cubeat alongside other hardware sequencers and the Yamaha C1 Music Computer, which was a DOS-based PC that had eight built-in MIDI ports and ran the Voyetra Sequencer. The C1 was used live as the master sequencer for the band's 1991 world tour to support *The Mix*, the first album done in the new digital studio.

How did you get involved with Steinberg?

We used Cubase more and more once it began running on Windows, and Steinberg continued to develop its "Virtual Studio Technology" step by step. Over time, we got to know the company, and since the middle of the 1990s, Henning [Schmitz] and I have had regular contact with the programmers at Steinberg and take part in the Cubase and Nuendo beta programs.

How is Cubase used in the studio?

Since the late 1990s, the VST environment of Cubase has been the center of our working studio, which we supplement with various pieces of special vintage equipment. The stability of the program and its many creative tools gives us the feel of a professional work environment. New tools like Groove Agent One and LoopMash, with its possibilities of interaction between audio tracks, are now being used in our creative process, although our work is not mainly based on audio loops.

The first album produced mainly in Cubase VST was *Tour de France Soundtracks*, which was released in the summer of 2003 for the 100th anniversary of the legendary cycling race. We did the mix through a digital mixing console, but everything else—the audio and MIDI tracks, including the controller data—was recorded in Cubase. There was a master desktop computer connected via VST System Link to laptop computers running VST instruments.

What role does Cubase play in producing your live albums?

The world tour we did to support *Tour de France Soundtracks* in 2004 was recorded in Cubase via a Yamaha 02R96 and a 16-channel RME Digiface audio interface. These live recordings were then mixed back at Kling Klang Studios using the new 5.1 surround features in Cubase SX2.

After preselecting a great amount of recorded material for possible use on the album, we used the archiving feature in Cubase to minimize the final tracks we selected and transfer them to another computer. From there, Henning and I could work in parallel on the different versions and formats: each version in German and international language and in two-channel and 5.1 surround versions. This ended up being released as the *Minimum-Maximum* CD, DVD, and SACD, probably one of the first Cubase 5.1 releases.

The Cubase surround panner and mixing automation made it possible to do this without an external mixing console or other hardware. It was the first Kling Klang product produced completely with VST technology. Today, we mix everything inside the computer with the help of the Steinberg CC121, the M-Audio ProjectMix in Cubase control mode, a JazzMutant Dexter touch screen controller, and others.

How is Cubase used in your live performance setup?

We started using Cubase live on stage in the Cubase SX version running on Windows XP. We felt [that configuration] was suitable to use live because of its stability, flexibility, and timing accuracy. The stage setup consisted of just four connected Sony

VAIO laptops, each one playing a different technical or musical part, and a 16-meter-wide video screen across the back. In 2002, we did our first live shows on the *Minimum-Maximum* world tour at the Cité de la Musique auditorium in Paris using this configuration. We were using specially designed, custom-built controller desks to play the first generation of VST instruments like [Steinberg's] HALion, Native Instruments Battery 1 and Kontakt 1, as well as a lot of the things built into Cubase, like the reverb, delays, modulation plug-ins, and also the A1 Virtual Analog Synthesizer. Some of the instruments, especially Kontakt, already had highly developed MIDI control features for almost every parameter, which helped us create and manipulate sounds in real time onstage. The peripheral hardware we use currently is pretty reduced: some MIDI controllers from Doepfer Regelwerk, Pocket Electronics, and M-Audio, as well as a multichannel RME audio interface.

What features are important when performing live?

Besides the advantage of easily transporting the equipment, the fact that we could use our studio projects directly on stage with only a few slight changes was important. The way the user interface works and the option to create screensets, toolbar presets, and the ability to define specific key commands are all useful for live performance as much or even more as in the studio.

Also, Cubase has features that make it possible for us to use four connected systems, which can be quite complex, and synchronize everything together onstage. Since 2008 we have also used a fifth computer with Cubase as a host for the vocoder plug-ins. Cubase has very flexible routing and MIDI filtering capabilities, which prevents certain plug-ins from reacting to controller data that is not meant for them, and makes it possible to use one physical MIDI connection for many different purposes. This really decreases the number of cables and interfaces needed onstage.

The synchronization features in Cubase play an important role, as we have the option to route MIDI time code to different outs at the same time together with MIDI clock. The use of VST System Link in addition to the MIDI synchronization keeps the timing between the different laptops very tight—sample accurate. And lastly, Cubase creates the master time code for the software video player and the MIDI events for the lighting desk, bringing everything you see and hear in our shows together in perfect sync.

What features would you like to see in the future?

As live playing has become a much bigger part of musicians' activities during the last 10 or 15 years, there should be even more importance [placed] on that. For example, a playlist for a quicker and easier song change and a synchronized note board would be helpful. For those features we have additional custom-made solutions based on MAX/MSP by Cycling '74. But not *everything* around Kraftwerk has to involve cycling!

CHRIS "THE GREEK" PANAGHI— PRODUCER, ENGINEER, DJ
New York, NY

Chris "The Greek" Panaghi is a producer, engineer, DJ, and head of A&R for Amathus Music. From early on in his career, Panaghi has embraced technology and produced electronic music for a variety of sources, from his own Top Five *Billboard* dance music hits to remixes for top artists like Michael Jackson, Gloria Estefan, Celine Dion, and Yoko Ono. In addition to producing and remixing, he runs his own recording studio and record label.

Looking at your discography, you work a lot! How has Cubase helped?

I've just been so busy. You know, the change in the music industry now with the influx of more indie labels, and outside of having the studio and producing, I'm busy remixing, and sometimes have to get two records done in a week. The beauty of Cubase's ability to recall something in a couple of seconds as opposed to having a big analog console and spending a day to recall is great. I just don't have the time.

How long have you used Cubase?

It's gotta be about 11 years. By now, I have no reason to look at anything else. It works great. It's got the features I need and the ability to use a lot of VST products. Whether it's my Steinberg stuff like Virtual Guitarist or third-party VSTs, I have what I need. I love my HALion, and I have tons and tons of sample libraries. The great thing for me is I've gone back to my old libraries from the last 20 years and converted them and set them up in HALion. It's phenomenal because all of my old analog samples and sounds, bits and nuggets that I've made, are now in my HALion library.

Do you remember which version you started with?

Yeah, it was Cubase VST 5. I've now made over 200 records, and I would say a good half of that was done in what I call my "Steinberg decade."

What attracted you to Cubase back then?

Well, I came from Voyetra. I was on Voyetra Sequencer Plus Gold on a DOS system, because I've been a PC guy my whole life. Back then, what I used to do, which was very head-turning in the late '80s and early '90s, was have two PCs locked through SMPTE time code. Originally, I was striping from Voyetra to tape. But then it was like, "Well, screw it—why don't I just sync it up to another PC with another program called SAW [Software Audio Workshop]?" Coming from that, the only thing for me that needed to be upgraded was the fact that with MIDI happening it was a bit archaic, but the ability to integrate digital audio, which was evolving so fast, just wasn't cutting it on my system. So I made the jump to Cubase VST.

Your perspective is different than guys coming from the straight analog world, where VST was very comfortable for them.

Yeah, for me it was a bit different. I made 80 records on my Voyetra-based system. So it wasn't like I was dabbling. As soon as I started, I went headfirst into the computer and didn't look back. Some of my big records, from Michael Jackson on down, were done on that system. Once my name started growing and things started happening, it's hard to stop in the middle of something and all of a sudden learn something completely different.

I've always had an analog desk, so when I saw Cubase, I could definitely [relate] to it. Here's a fader, here's an EQ, and it kind of mimicked it. But back then it was nowhere near the level it's at now.

Over the course of 200 records, where has your focus been musically?

It's actually been a bit of everything. I'm an active songwriter. I'm always looking to build my catalog, whether it's going to be for artists that I'm affiliated with or pitching to others. I also produce and remix in many genres. Even though I specialize in electronic dance music and stuff, I do a lot of other things to branch out and stay diverse. Recording jazz or classical music is a different approach than doing electronic dance, but the principles remain the same.

What's your studio setup?

The norm these days is to have a project studio, but I'm one of those guys that have a lot more than a basic project studio in my home. I do one to two records a week, depending on if it's a single or an EP, or doing an album where I block out a month of time. That said, I don't really need to book out my studio because I'm so busy with my own work.

As far as my rig goes, I have a 64-input D&R Triton console with full automation, even though it's not hooked up now because there's really no need for it with Cubase. I still have all my decks: my Tascam DA-30s and everything else, even though I haven't touched them in about seven years. I've sold off any extra equipment I've had, two-inch machines and stuff. I have an arsenal of keyboards, synths, and outboard gear. I have my fun analog gear like my Urei LA4.

More and more, I'm working inside the computer, and that's been the biggest change in the last five to seven years. I find myself going less and less to my keyboard synths like my vintage Juno-106 or my Roland JV-1080. I've either sampled them or I'm using plug-ins that are similar. I love The Grand. I think it's a killer piano sound, and I haven't used my Yamaha Motif for piano in a while.

What is your hardware front end for Cubase?

I run a very beefed-up PC: a quad core with 4 GB of RAM, with three SATA terabyte hard drives. I have three MOTU 2408 audio interfaces with 24 tracks going into the desk, which stays at zero. I use a Steinberg Midex 8 interface for MIDI. I have the Universal Audio UAD-1 power plug-in card set up in my PC and a TC Electronics PowerCore, both beefed up with a lot of plug-ins.

Do you mix in the box or use the console or a controller?

I do everything right inside Cubase. If I have to run something out and back in for a certain effect I'll do it, but lately I haven't touched much outboard gear. That's a big thing for me, since I've always been a big analog guy. Every dance record I've done I've used a Juno-106 for a bass line or things like that, and some of my go-to things like a BBE Sonic Maximizer on a kick drum or a Urei LA4 on a bass line I'm not using anymore. It says a lot.

Most of the analog gear has been modeled or emulated as well.

And they sound great! The quality level has really come up. If you look at now versus 10 years ago, there's no way you could have A/B'ed them. To me, there's no such thing as the analog-to-digital comparison anymore. I think it's pretty much gone out the window. When you listen to music in general, whether it's radio, on TV, or anything else, it's all digital. You're talking about a generation now where iTunes has the biggest market share, and no one is walking around with a Sony Walkman anymore. It's all iPods. When you start to look at the compression ratios on that, analog doesn't even matter anymore. It's not really about that.

You mentioned large sample libraries you've recorded. How important is that to electronic music?

To me, that's everything. You need a good sound library, not just third-party sound libraries that you can buy, but your own arsenal of sounds. To me, that's what defines your sound. I'm fortunate enough that I've invested in many vintage pieces of equipment, like a [Roland] TR-808 or TR-909, so if I want to make some killer drum sounds, I take my TR-909 and physically sample it. It isn't like back in the day where I'd be throwing it into my Akai S950, 100, or 3000—now it goes right into Cubase. But along the way, I might run it through my Urei LA4 or things like that. Once I have it recorded, I can do things in Cubase base like Bit Crush it a little bit, or do some other things to make it a little dirty, but at least the sound coming in has an analog feel.

I don't think a lot of people are doing that these days. What I think they're doing is just opening up a box, taking a kick drum and saying, "OK, that's cool." Throwing some compression on it and that's it.

What are some of your go-to features in Cubase?

One of my favorites is Bit Crusher. Cubase has some great effects that come within the program. The delays and reverbs are good. Are they superior? No, but they're good. Some of the overdrives are absolutely killer! When you start putting those kinds of processors on loops, it's outstanding. I think it has changed the whole dynamic 100 percent, especially for electronic music.

How do you organize your massive sound libraries?

I firmly believe that if you're not organized from day one, you're not ever going to be organized! I'm like that, with the studio being neat and not being able to see a cable anywhere, down to organization in the filing system. I have three drives. The C drive holds all the programs. Then I have two drives for audio samples, with everything broken down into folders. For example, I have a folder called "Chris the Greek Kicks 1." So when I open up HALion, I'm gonna have 72 kicks spread across the keyboard to audition. I have these templates set up for everything: snares, claps, cymbals, or whatever.

It gets a little tricky when I do pitched instruments. Obviously, I have to make sure they're spread out across the keyboard and tuned right. But for what I call "one-shots" and loops, it's easy enough to call it up in HALion or to just bring it into the Project window and set your markers and time expand it. It probably sounds ghetto, but to me it's completely natural.

I think that's the beauty of the system, working in ways that make sense to you.

Exactly. If you're sitting in a session, the one thing that can ruin the creativity is if you're looking for a sound and you can't find it. You hear it in your head or have the idea, you start to look for it, and before you know it 15 or 20 minutes has gone by and you've forgotten what you're doing. It sucks.

Do you do most of your work in-house?

I'm fortunate enough that everything I do, I do in my own place. I don't really like working outside of my own environment. My studio is tuned. It's a blueprinted room. It's dead-on. It isn't like I just took a spare bedroom; it's a full-floated room that I set up from the beginning when I built the house.

How do you collaborate with other artists?

Lately the way it works is if someone's not here and wants to listen to it, an MP3 is sent over AIM, AOL Instant Messenger, or MSN Messenger. I had a situation where my keyboardist moved from the New York area out to Pennsylvania, and for about six months we worked in that fashion. I'd send him, say, the drums and vocals locked to a grid, and he would do his keyboard part and send me back the MIDI files. Then I'd have my own sounds here and figure out what I wanted to use and what I didn't. The Internet has made that more accessible.

How about delivery to the label?

I'm still old school. I always like to make sure that a CD goes out. Lately, I have to say the trend is to send a link, like YouSendIt. That's been the consensus unless someone has an FTP site where I just upload it.

Do you have any techniques that you've come up with that suit the way you work?

I use Cubase in conjunction with SoundForge. Let me explain that a little further. Let's say I'm tracking vocals. I'll track my vocals and comp them in Cubase, then bounce them as stems over to SoundForge, clean them up, tune them, and reimport them back into Cubase. I find this works better for me to clean up dirty tracks with background noises and things like that. At the end of the day, I'm going to be using the stems to be sent out for remixes or anything else, so it's easy enough just to have them started that way.

That's the beauty of a computer-based system — its flexibility to work how you want to work.

I get e-mails all the time from guys that want to make music and ask me if they have to have Pro Tools. And my answer is always, "There is no single way to make music." I know guys still making music with MPCs. I used Voyetra for a good nine years. I know guys that are doing things in ways where people would look at them like they're crazy! You don't need any one specific thing to make music. Technology has made it even better. Bottom line, it's whatever you're comfortable with.

25 Years of Steinberg

Steinberg officially turns 25 years old in 2009, a remarkable milestone in the history of any company. Along with this longevity, Steinberg has amassed a huge user base over the past two-and-half decades, in part due to its consistent innovation in creating new standards for the computer recording industry, and in part due to its willingness and ability to adapt and provide tools for new genres of music and customers. In this chapter, we'll take a look back at how Steinberg developed as a company, the technical achievements it brought to the table, and hear from some of the key players who made the company what it is today.

Steinberg Media Technologies AG headquarters near Hamburg, Germany

CHRONOLOGY AND TECHNOLOGICAL ACHIEVEMENTS

1983 Manfred Rürup and Karl "Charlie" Steinberg meet in Hamburg, Germany, at a recording session.

1984 Steinberg and Rürup officially found Steinberg Research GmbH and release the Pro-16, a basic multitrack MIDI sequencer built for the Commodore 64 computer using a homemade MIDI interface.

Steinberg Pro-16 for the Commodore C64 computer

1985 Steinberg releases the Pro-24, a 24-track MIDI sequencer for the Atari ST with a built-in MIDI interface and new features such as scoring, quantization, and MIDI editing.

1986 Steinberg releases Pro-24 for the Atari Amiga.

1987 Steinberg releases Pro-24 III and the SMP24 SMPTE/MIDI Processor. The company is renamed Steinberg Soft- und Hardware GmbH.

1988 Steinberg/Jones opens for distribution in the US market.

Steinberg Pro-24 for Amiga

1989 Steinberg releases Cubit for the Atari, which becomes Cubase, the first MIDI sequencer to feature a graphical display of musical information. The company also develops for the Topaz hard disk recorder and MIMIX automation system.

1990 Steinberg releases Cubase 2.0, adding support for the Apple Macintosh. The company also releases Cubeat, a scaled-down version of Cubase.

1991 Steinberg releases Cubase Audio for the Mac, adding audio recording, editing, and mixing alongside MIDI. The company also releases Time Bandit, a time-stretching and pitch-shifting program for the Mac.

Steinberg Cubase 1.0

1992 Steinberg releases Cubase 3.0, Cubase for Windows, Cubase Lite, and Tango, a jamming application. Steinberg partners with Yamaha to develop Cubase Audio for the Yamaha CBX-D5 music computer.

1993 Steinberg releases Cubase Score for Windows, featuring score printing, and a GM/GS editor. The company also releases Cubase Audio for Windows and Atari Falcon.

1994 Steinberg releases the MusicStation Digital Studio Kit, featuring auto accompaniment and backing track creation, and founds Spectral Design GmbH to develop plug-in effects.

Steinberg Tango

Steinberg WaveLab 1.0

Steinberg Cubase VST for Mac

Steinberg LM4 VST Instrument

1995 Steinberg releases WaveLab, a dedicated audio editor for Windows, and ReCycle, a sample-editing tool developed by Propellerhead Software.

1996 Steinberg releases Cubase VST (Virtual Studio Technology) for Mac, featuring a real-time studio environment including EQ, effects, mixing, and automation.

1997 Steinberg releases Cubase VST for Windows. VST and ASIO are released as open standards to allow third-party manufacturers to develop plug-ins and audio hardware. Steinberg also releases the second Propellerhead-designed product, ReBirth.

1998 Steinberg releases Cubase VST 4 for Mac and WaveLab 2.

1999 Steinberg releases Cubase VST 4.1, featuring VST 2.0 technology, which adds virtual instrument plug-ins to the VST environment. The company also releases the ASIO 2.0 protocol.

2000 Steinberg releases Nuendo, a digital audio workstation built for surround sound and incorporating features for professional post-production and multimedia. Nuendo-branded hardware developed by RME is released to complete the system. Steinberg Soft- und Hardware GmbH is renamed Steinberg Media Technologies AG.

2001 Steinberg releases HALion and The Grand, two high-quality virtual instruments based on sampling technology, as well as the Houston Controller and MIDEX 8 MIDI Interface, featuring Steinberg's Linear Time Base (LTB) technology.

2002 Steinberg releases Cubase SX, a new version of Cubase written from the ground up with new code, as well as the Warp VST and Virtual Guitarist guitar plug-ins, WaveLab 4.0, WaveLab Essential, the MIDEX 3 MIDI Interface, Nuendo Time Base Synchronizer, and VST System Link, a new technology for the synchronization of audio computer systems across a network.

Steinberg Cubase SX 1.0

2003 Steinberg is acquired by Pinnacle Systems and releases Cubase SX2 and Nuendo 2.0. Also released is the HALion String Edition Volume 1, D'cota VST Synthesizer, Xphraze Phrase VST Synthesizer, Waldorf Edition Synthesizer, HALion 2.0, V-Stack, and Groove Agent, a virtual drum machine.

2004 Steinberg releases Cubase SX3, Cubase SE, Nuendo 3, Nuendo DTS Encoder, WaveLab 5, HALion 3, and Hypersonic. Steinberg also combines software and hardware in integrated packages, the Cubase System|2 and Cubase System|4.

Steinberg Nuendo 1.0

2005 Yamaha Corporation acquires Steinberg from Pinnacle Systems and develops Studio Connections for better hardware/software integration. Cubase SE 3, Hypersonic 2, Groove Agent 2, The Grand 2, Virtual Bassist, and HALion String Edition 2 are released. ASIO technology is updated to version 2.1.

2006 Steinberg releases Cubase 4, featuring VST 3 technology, as well as WaveLab 6, Virtual Guitarist 2, HALion Symphonic Orchestra, Groove Agent 3, and a hardware synchronizer for Nuendo. ASIO technology is updated to version 2.2.

Steinberg WaveLab 6.0

2007 Steinberg releases Sequel, an entry-level music-creation application. Also released are Nuendo 4 and Cubase Essential 4.

Steinberg Cubase 5

2008 Steinberg releases its first hardware co-developed with Yamaha, the MR816X and MR816CSX FireWire interfaces, and the CC121 USB controller, and dubs their direct link with Cubase "Advanced Integration." The company also releases Cubase 4.5, Sequel 2, and the VST3 Software Development Kit (SDK). Steinberg acquires from Syncrosoft the eLicenser technology used to copy-protect Cubase.

2009 Steinberg releases Cubase 5, The Grand 3, and the CI2, a portable USB audio interface and controller co-developed with Yamaha.

In Their Own Words—
AN INTERVIEW WITH STEINBERG VETERAN AND DIRECTOR OF MARKETING FRANK SIMMERLEIN

How long have you been with Steinberg?

In the beginning I was a freelancer doing work for Steinberg, but it's been more than 20 years. Which makes me a dinosaur, so to speak.

How did you get involved with the company?

I've been a musician all my life, and in the early days I worked as a marketing guy in an advertising agency. I knew someone from a music shop here in Hamburg where I bought my keyboards, called M-Town, who was the marketing guy for Steinberg in those days. I was reading *Keyboards* magazine, a German music magazine, and I saw a really bad advertisement for Steinberg. Really, it was home desktop publishing at its worst. At that time I worked at an ad agency and had several other types of clients, from razors to sausages, and I thought it would be good to have a high-tech company as well. So, I just gave [Steinberg] a call and told them that the ad looked awful. "If this is a professional product, it needs professional marketing." That's when that marketing guy brought Manfred Rürup into the advertising agency. And that is how I got them as a client.

And how did you come to be in-house?

I was responsible for Steinberg in that agency for two years. Then I left the agency. And the moment I left, Manfred asked me if I could still work for him, at least as a freelancer. So I did. I was working as a musician and had a lot of marketing experience already, working for years in agencies. Then I put more into making music, but in parallel I started working for Manfred and his company. Then, out of one meeting per month came one meeting per week. And then it started as four half days, and it ended up at seven full days per week. So even if it was on a freelance basis for many years, I was part of Steinberg.

And what aspects of marketing were you doing at the time?

I took over more and more. In those days, Manfred's former wife was a designer as well. I worked at Steinberg with her before she left the company. It was very typical of a small company, where we had very little resources for marketing. Then as it became bigger and bigger, we needed more resources, and today we are like a full-service agency within Steinberg. We do everything. We have everything here from copywriters and designers to Web and film concepts.

Being a musician, how much did you get involved with the product itself long the way?

There was a time when I did everything on the GUI, from Cubase VST to the first Nuendo versions, instruments like the Model E, LM4, PPG, and all these synthesizers. I've done millions of these plug-in interfaces. I did HALion. HALion was born in a Greek restaurant across the street.

VST was something special between Charlie Steinberg and myself. He had all these ideas about VST, and he started programming, and then he called me and said, "Frank, I need the graphics. I need a surface, an interface." That is where the whole thing started.

There were no restrictions because it was native audio, so I was able to develop an interface that was certainly unseen by the world.

It was a revolution, so to speak: native audio with this new look. I have to admit, the way we dealt with the interface sometimes was not very good. It was not always easy to deal with it. But people understood what it was all about. They know analog hardware from the studio—this is a mixer, this is a reverb, delay, and so on. And it was so much easier for them to understand how routing all these things worked in VST. I think that was the main reason for its success.

If you look at it today, it looks very outdated. But if you look at a car that is 10 years old, it looks old too. So does VST. But then, it was new to the world. I remember when I was in the US at a music shop shortly after VST was released. There was a guy looking at a huge VST poster on the wall. I told him that we had done that, and he said he loved VST because he was working eight hours a day looking at it and it looks somehow beautiful, it gives something to him. I found that very interesting.

Was the development of VST a long process?

I think in all it was developed over about six months. Charlie worked like crazy. If you have a revolution, it's quite often very fast. The real revelation for me in those days came when I was sitting in my real studio at home, with a mixing desk and all these things, and I was sitting in front of Cubase in the early VST days. I looked at it and said, "I need this. I need a button here, I need mono to be here, and this, and this, and this." And then I started painting in a graphics program things that didn't exist yet. I would shuffle that over to Charlie, and he would do the coding over the picture. So it would work both ways. Sometimes he would come to me and need an interface for what he had programmed, and sometimes I came back to him with a graphical representation and nothing behind it.

Were there any challenges in moving from Pro-24 to Cubase?

Pro-24 was more pattern oriented. It would run from top to bottom; one pattern box on top of another. Cubase was more tape oriented. If a tape is rolling, it's rolling from right to left. And the interesting thing was you had to rethink the way you work. I had used Pro-24 for some time and done several big jobs on it, so I was used to it. Cubase was something I had to learn, even though it was a lot more logical. It was like a tape, from right to left; you can cut it, and you can move it. It's like we Western people read. But it took some time to make the jump from the top-down approach to the right-left approach. And after a few days of working with Cubase, I couldn't imagine working in the old way ever again.

Was there a vision of having a full studio in the computer from the beginning?

Not in the beginning. When I think about how we started, the programs at that time could do very little. Yet it was so amazing at the time. Charlie was a musician, and he started programming because he needed certain things at that time. But I'm not sure if we had a vision of where this would end up today or we had the imagination of what it could be at the time. That was a process that grew over time.

I remember when the synthesizers first had MIDI. I had the Atari and the Pro-24 with MIDI, and I could do a program change without touching the synthesizer. Unbelievable! We laugh about it now, but it was unbelievable. You could tell the Pro-24 to change the program on the synthesizer from number 18 to number 19, and the bloody thing would do it! It was revolutionary at that time.

It was a long process. It was with Cubase Audio XT that we were able to integrate Digidesign hardware. I think this was when the idea for a full studio was really growing.

What do you see as the biggest single innovation in Steinberg's history?

I think Cubase in itself in the beginning was revolutionary: that way of working. You could even say today that the concept of Cubase, the record and playback itself, still has a lot in common with the first Cubase version. It still has some similarity.

The second revolution was when audio could be recorded. My first audio sequencer with Cubase was an audio card where I could have two tracks of audio. Unbelievable!

In the end I do see VST as the biggest step because it's more than just, for example, a reverb. VST is so much more. VST instruments is an entire industry today. If you look for example at the Arturia package, that has everything they make in it: the CS-80, Prophet, and all the Moog stuff. I had a lot of this stuff in the past in real hardware, and today it's just in one package. This would not be possible if we hadn't come up with VST. If you look at Cubase 5 today, it would not be possible without VST.

What are some of the big challenges Steinberg has faced?

I think the biggest challenge was that the hardware and the processors couldn't follow our ideas in terms of power. The CPUs and all these things are always late. You have so many ideas, and you want to develop things further.

The first Cubase version was running on an Atari, which was running at something like 65 MHz, and it was too slow. Then came VST on the first PowerPCs, which were fantastic at the time but still not powerful enough. As long as I've been with the company, the computers were never fast enough. So, these days we have more cores, which is how the computer industry tried to overcome the problem, but more cores doesn't help in the end if the system bus is too slow. Working with more cores and trying to push all the data through the same bus doesn't work.

Of course, today's computer systems are better than a complete hardware-based DSP system. You can have more audio tracks, and the algorithm behind the audio engine is a lot more intelligent and can work dynamically.

That's what I think is the biggest challenge even today. Will there someday be a computer that really delivers the full power we need? Today, I'm on my seventh or eighth computer, and over time the machines are getting faster and faster. But I'm still able to make the machine hit the wall if I like. The Intels of the world must love us, because we need faster processors to keep it going. You don't need another core for a Word document, but for music or cutting movies and so on, you always need more.

Is it harder to make bigger leaps forward with each version, or are we less impressed by new things these days?

I think both are true. It's definitely not that easy to surprise people, because expectations are so high. If you look at REVerence, for example, that's something that could easily be sold as a convolution reverb for $300 to $500, but it comes with the product. Groove Agent One, LoopMash, or Beat Designer could all be things on their own. On this side, it's getting more and more difficult.

I think it was around 10 or 12 years ago, I remember one afternoon when one of the earlier VST versions was being released, and I was talking with Manfred. It was a sunny afternoon, the sun was shining in his office window, and we were sitting there, and said, "Wow, what's next? What could anyone want after this? Is this the end of the product?" It was so difficult to imagine at that time that there was so much more to develop. I think we hadn't released VST instruments yet, so there was much more to come.

I think this way of thinking could happen to you all the time. To think, "There is no more we can do with the product." If I have learned one thing over the years, it's that this is never true. The next version usually has some feature in it that we couldn't imagine surviving without it all these years before. If I look at all the things that are in Cubase 5, it will happen again.

In Their Own Words—
AN INTERVIEW WITH STEINBERG FOUNDERS KARL "CHARLIE" STEINBERG AND MANFRED RÜRUP

What part of Germany are you from, Charlie?

Charlie Steinberg: I was born in Westphalia [close to Muenster, Dortmund, Essen], which is very different, but they say Hamburg is the gateway to the world, because of the harbor and everything, so my plans were reaching far wider than Hamburg. I was thinking of maybe going to Australia or something. But I got stuck here when I met Manfred. [*Laughs*] Which isn't a bad thing at all.

Why did you come to Hamburg?

CS: My band was recording close to Hamburg, and that's actually where I met Manfred, in that studio. And that's where it all started, if you like. I recorded with my band, and then they took me on as an engineer, because I was there very often and it was totally out in the country with nothing around it, where you could only work and sleep. Which is kind of ideal, in a way. And then Manfred had some music, and record companies got interested in it, and he was supposed to record it there. And that's where we met.

Manfred was working at M-Town, which was a big music store here. So he was always bringing the big gear with him, like the first samplers: the E-mu 2 and Synergy, if you remember that one. That was a crazy machine! And the sequencer stuff began to happen with the Oberheim and stuff like that. We did a lot of triggering and gates and all this stuff, too. We immediately had a connection.

What instrument do you play?

CS: I come from the guitar, but I play keyboard mainly.

And Manfred?

CS: Manfred is an excellent keyboardist. He used to be a very well-known studio keyboardist, actually. He's really good.

So that's how I got involved in some other projects that he did. I didn't know anybody in Hamburg, so I immediately got into the studio scene, and there weren't too many engineers around, so I had some good gigs in larger studios, which was very good to learn all this stuff.

Actually, at that very studio where we met, we already began with the C64 [Commodore 64 computer]. Manfred had an American *Keyboard* magazine, and in that magazine the MIDI format was explained. And that got me thinking, because it seemed so easy, and I had just started with computers. So that's how it started.

Were you working with hardware sequencers at the time?

CS: Yeah, right. We had the Oberheim drums, and they had a sequencer—a very complicated device. Don't ask me for the name. And Manfred used to operate it; I never had a clue, actually. But, you know, it was all about triggering, gates and signals, and putting that in the patch bay. We had a Pro-1 and the Prophet, and they could be triggered, as well as the drum machines. The clocking was tricky—one had the Roland type of DIN and the other had something different. It was very interesting. So we did a lot of experimenting, like with the sampler—the E-mu 2 was one of the first I saw—we started to sample things like crazy; glass bowls or anything that was laying around.

And how did the computer come into play?

CS: I didn't like computers initially, because I was a bit into electronics—I did my own boards and soldering, and it never actually worked, but I tried to invent things. I built a synthesizer in, I think, 1978. It was a big thing—a big board behind a panel with knobs. And that was an interesting thing because it had 16 faders, so you could actually make a waveform or you could run it for triggering or for providing pitch information if you ran it very slow. But you could run it very fast, and then it had a waveform of its own. I remember sitting there and listening. Anyway, I was into that kind of stuff, and I thought *computers*—I mean it's just a little board with a hex keyboard and a hex display and, well, what's that good for?

But then the ZX-81 came. It's a little Sinclair computer. Later they had the Spectrum, which was the color version, and then came the C64. I thought immediately that it's kind of soldering without the soldering—you can just type in the commands, and it will do the connections automatically. I understood the idea of all these TTL switches and how it basically worked.

Again, it coincided with this MIDI stuff that was starting to happen, and we thought it would be very simple to record that into the memory and play it back. The studio we were at was a million-deutschmark studio, so we couldn't afford much time, and that's why it was so interesting for us to have a recording machine. Multitrack recording was just not affordable. Plus, you could edit the recording and quantize it, pitch it—amazing stuff!

Then the [Yamaha] DX7 happened, which was a perfect fit for this. It had only one MIDI channel and was not multitimbral at that time, but you could program the oscillators and modulators such that you had very different sounds in the lower and the higher range, so you could create some sort of multitrack. Add a drum machine and, wow; you had a piece of music coming out of this machine. Amazing!

How did the introduction of the Atari ST advance the technology?

CS: Manfred initially played with his band live on stage, and he came around quite a bit; he went to the music stores and showed people this stuff, and only a very few actually got it. But the Atari had a buzz about it a long time before it was released, just because it had MIDI ports. And everybody was saying this was the greatest thing on earth, although nobody knew anything about it. The good thing was that Atari was giving the developers very early machines and documentation. The documentation really had little to do with what was going on in the machine, so you really had to be very creative in that respect. We got another guy named Werner Kracht, who is still with the company, and he actually started the Pro-24, and it had a graphical user interface, which was amazing because the only other thing that did was the Macintosh, and that wasn't affordable at all—very expensive in Europe at that time.

So as far back as the Pro-24 there was a graphic interface?

CS: Yeah, it was kind of a clone of the Mac II or something. And it took off quite reasonably.

When did you officially become a company?

CS: I think 1984. That was called Steinberg Research.

Did you have a background in computers or electrical engineering?

CS: No. I used to study music, but didn't follow that through. Actually, the sound engineering got in between. Playing guitar, I was always more interested in the technology than the instrument.

How did you settle on the name "Steinberg"?

CS: It was kind of a joke. I think I said it. I'm not sure. "Steinberg Research—hey, that sounds cool! And the Americans will especially love it. They love these kinds of names." On one hand it's like Steinway, on the other it's like Einstein, you know.

What was it like trying to sell such a new concept in the early days?

MANFRED RÜRUP: I was a musician, but couldn't make a living from it, so I worked in Hamburg in a music retail shop. And because of that I always went to the Musikmesse in Frankfurt, and the synthesizer area was happening, so I had some contact into the retail scene, which helped.

I was on tour and took my C64 portable computer, which was called the SX64. And every morning where we were touring I went to the music stores—Berlin, Cologne, all these places—and would show them our product: the Pro-16. And the response was not so good. They didn't know what this was all about. But then we started selling the products: we packed them, shipped them, and did everything ourselves. I think the biggest problem was that you had to determine the price for the product, which for the people was just a disk—a floppy disk at that time. Which has a value of only 50¢ or something. And people would ask why they should pay hundreds of dollars for just a floppy disk. So we had to give it value.

So the idea of intellectual property was new to them?

MR: Yes, absolutely. When we started to do distribution and we went to Frankfurt—which is a great place for startup companies, much more than for established companies—we met all these people who came up to us and wanted to do distribution. We didn't know these guys. But we had good luck because we went to England, and in England they started very soon to give the product value. They noticed much more that this product needed a higher value to really become a success. So the English price was always about twice what it was over here in Germany. So that was one of the biggest problems—and copy protection.

Copy protection was an issue even back then?

MR: Yes, from the beginning. I remember a time when we had copy protection on a floppy disk where you took a needle and you put some holes into the floppy disk. Then you copied the program onto that disk and because you've got these little holes in there, the machine read the disk in blocks. So when it's copied and you suddenly can't read these blocks, then you know it's a copy. This was the original idea.

Unfortunately, the machine made a horrible noise when it was trying to read these blocks, you know, which were totally broken. So people called up, of course, and said, "What's going on with this program? It's making such a horrible noise! It's destroying my computer!" Back then we had to share a lot of jobs, and I was doing the tech support, so I had all these mad people on the phone driving me nuts. [*Laughs*]

CS: As Manfred said, you have this cheap disk, so people would say, "Let's just copy it."

MR: And of course the dealers always said to me they were not going to sell the product because "I'm only going to sell it once." So we told them it was copy protected. "Yeah, right," and then they already had a copy there, you know? They didn't want to spend the time demonstrating the product and then find that the guy already had a copy. Then the dealer works for nothing. It's been a problem since day one.

Was it difficult to demo the product in those days? You couldn't just bring in your laptop like you can today.

MR: The dealers all had systems, but most were not running. The interfacing wasn't correct, and we're only talking about MIDI, but even with MIDI there was Omni and Poly mode, and all the old synthesizers were not really clear on what mode they were running in. Sequential Circuits, for example, didn't support MIDI, Oberheim had their own system, and only Roland was, I think, working perfectly, and then Yamaha was using that protocol.

What also made it hard was people didn't really know what to do with that stuff. When you look at that time, people had drum machines and they had some hardware sequencers. But they didn't know what to do with the computer and software on it. I thought that scoring would be a great thing to do on it — notes and all that. That's what people thought would really make sense.

Did the early products have scoring?

MR: No, that came much later.

CS: Oh, we had scoring on the C64.

MR: Kind of. [*Laughs*]

CS: Technically, it's the most incredible thing you've ever seen! [*More laughter*] But yes, that's true. The notion at the time was scoring, and also doing like a Bach dicing thing, you know? Computer music — you press a button and it plays a song.

MR: But most of the stuff in the beginning you could only do straight notes — quarter notes, 16th notes. You couldn't do triplets, for example. So from a programming point of view it was very limiting. It was hard to program on hardware sequencers as well. Did you ever work on a hardware sequencer? It was a pain in the ass. You really had to count a lot. Push a button three times. Push a button six times. Push a button 12 times, and if you did something wrong you had to start from scratch. Look at the Roland TB-303, or something like that — it's really hard to program.

After the Pro-24 came Cubase. When was that?

CS: Cubase was in 1989. Up until then, we didn't have anything to do with Macs or PCs. It was just too much work, and the Atari was working, so it took a while to develop Cubase. Cubase is kind of a front end to the Pro-24, if you like. The Pro-24 was just a panel, like a multitrack recorder, so you had the record-enable buttons and all that, but you couldn't really see any of the music like you do today. I think we were the first to do it like that; a graphic display of parts and a timeline. I'm still wondering if video editors or something at that time would have existed that did a similar thing.

We really thought a long time about how we could help people deal with musical data. And that's what came out, and it's pretty much what we have today.

And where does the name "Cubase" come from?

CS: I remember it was very, very difficult to find a name, because everything you would think of was somehow covered already. Initially, we called it Cubit, but the French said you can't do that because it's a very ugly word. So we called it Cubase. Really it was a matter of trying to find a name that was unique.

And the next breakthrough was the addition of audio recording?

CS: Yes, the next big thing was audio, of course. And also we started to make it portable, to get it over to the Mac. That's where Digidesign had TDM, the early Pro Tools system to record audio. They had an interface to control this system, and it was very tricky, because whenever you wanted to tell that engine, the DAE, to do something, you had to stop it first. It was a bit complicated and shaky. We weren't very happy with it, but we made a Mac program to interface with that audio engine.

The next thing was the CBXD5, which is a Yamaha device. They did that exclusively with us initially. Later it was opened up to others. They wanted to fight Digidesign, and they said, "This is a dumb machine; it's a SCSI disk, more or less; you give it SCSI commands to locate and record things." Apart from that, it had pretty good I/O, and we put a front end onto that. So we developed our own audio engine, which we later put with the Atari Falcon, which had built-in DSP. And so we could use that entire engine and even the plug-ins that we did for Pro Tools, and DSP code that could go directly to the Falcon. So we had that thing where we couldn't move parts with audio and record and everything, which we initially did for the Digidesign system. And then we did the audio part ourselves.

Because we now had this stuff on the Mac, I realized that there was this Sound Manager in OS 9, which is an API for programmers to speak to the internal audio hardware. That was a crucial point, as well as the introduction of the PowerPC. The first Mac I had was a 60 MHz PowerPC, but it was fast enough to do audio streaming. This made it possible for native audio on the Mac.

I was unhappy with the graphics, though. As a sound engineer I was used to having tight control of the VU meters, and things like that. And then Frank Simmerlein came along—he is the graphics guy for Steinberg, and still is today. And he said that he made something for the Digidesign DAE version, but they never took it. I looked at it and immediately put it in—it looked so great. Then I said, "You know, we might even do effects, this machine is so crazy fast. We could do some reverb, or at least chorus should be possible." And he freaked out, and said, "This is like a virtual studio." And that's where the name came from—VST (Virtual Studio Technology). And that pretty much came all at one time.

Did you always envision everything being contained in the computer, or did it come one piece at a time?

CS: I think we had that vision, yes. Because there was already, several years earlier, the HDR 4-track hard disk recording system, which was amazing—a very expensive and huge machine. And back then it was obvious to me that everything would be in one machine, and not only that, but the one important point which you tend to forget nowadays because it's very common, is the total recall thing. You could call up the file on our computer and everything was just like it was yesterday, which was totally amazing if you had been working on huge analog desks where you had to take photographs and write everything down and you would still never get it there again. And then the patch bay—you can't see anything. It's full of cables. How do you know what was connected? Write it down? You don't have the time.

When did you adopt the Steinberg slogan "Creativity First"?

CS: I think that was at the beginning of Cubase. It was an idea to make you less dependent on things that are very complicated. I think what's also interesting is the slogan we had before that: "Don't Stop the Music." It was because of this DAE thing, where everything you did would stop the machine. It's technically pretty tricky to keep things going and change things, because whenever you change something, it has to be dealt with. So we were pretty much the first, I think, to do that with audio. You could move things around and it would just play on. If you play something and you say, "Now give me the next chunk of data from the disk," but it has moved somewhere, the machine crashes. So, I thought that was a good slogan for that particular time. And then later came the creativity thing.

VST and ASIO were two big innovations; did they happen at the same time?

CS: ASIO was later. With VST, I kind of abstracted it a bit, and I don't really know how, but published it. It wasn't really supposed to take off, not at all. I didn't expect it. That's why it's also a bit clumsy. You would do it a bit cleaner if you had known what would happen, you know? So then, the students took on that, because the example that we had was just a gain knob, or just a generic interface. It was so easy to write for it, so it exploded. They wrote billions of plug-ins. That's how the VST thing took off.

ASIO (Audio Stream In/Out) was developed because we realized that everything was concentrated in this machine, and everything was an integrated system, and the only thing that is really around it is source code. It's all just software and nothing else. So the I/O was very tricky to deal with—we did an interface where we said, "Okay, this is a black box with inputs and outputs. Let's define what it should look like when transferring data." A lot of the stuff with Sound Manager was totally crazy—there was no synchronization between input and output. So we sat down and did ASIO, which just like VST is a very simple protocol. It was taken on by the hardware manufacturers, who were suffering from the problem that everything was done in software. And this led to these I/O devices, which are still very important today, of course.

The very first ASIO driver was a Sound Manager abstraction. ASIO was a good thing because it kept us from always having to reinvent the wheel.

Where did WaveLab come from?

CS: Well, we had these editors from the beginning, because all these sound modules needed editing. And that went on for quite a while. But WaveLab was a unique product because one guy wrote it: Philip Goutier. Basically, he's a Windows programmer, and he said that all of this stuff is so slow on Windows, but knowing how to deal with the Windows API, it's easy to make it very fast. That was the amazing thing about WaveLab initially — it was extremely fast, the waveforms and all that.

Did the company grow steadily or in big leaps when a new breakthrough happened?

MR: I think when the Atari came out it was really big growth then. When the Atari had the built-in MIDI interface everybody went crazy, much more over here than in America. I think in the US they only delivered the Atari with the color monitor, while over here they had the black-and-white monitor. And everybody over here, for some reason, thought that this was a serious machine, while in America people thought it was a game machine. Over here they saw it as a cheap Macintosh. It's black-and-white, the monitor looks a little more professional and all that stuff, so it was seen differently here than in America.

CS: I think up till then we were five people. From then on it exploded.

MR: It was the Atari, and then we brought it over to the Mac, and then the PC. Then came audio. Once native audio became big with VST, the company really exploded, in terms of people. We were not prepared for it, I think. When you think about it, everybody wanted to sing or play guitar into the computer a long time before. They didn't want to use MIDI. MIDI was okay, but what they really wanted to do was take their guitar and record. So how many times did they ask us at shows, "Where can I plug in my guitar?" Well sorry, you can't. But once that became possible, there was such a big, big push to the whole idea of using computers.

As the company grew after VST was released, did your role change at all?

CS: Basically we kept these roles all the time. Of course, I became a bit more involved in management issues, but basically I was always free to do development work. I think that was good, because the next step was VST instruments. And that was always, to me, a conclusion to what had happened before. That's where I continued to develop, and Manfred was driving the sales and was in the driver's seat.

We were supposed to become a listed [public] company, because the company was growing like hell and we were in a very good situation; sales were very good. So the bank people said we had to go public. So we got more people involved. It is a very long process, to become public, and it costs a hell of a lot of money. You have to do all the bookkeeping things differently and very expensively. Then, when we were at that point and the bank said everything looks very good, then the crash came. Then 9/11 came. And nobody wanted to do anything at all. That was shocking, because we had gone in that direction and spent a lot of money and acquired a lot of people. So that all went down, and it was very tough.

So then the next logical step was to sell the company?

CS: Yes. We sold it to Pinnacle Systems, and then later to Yamaha, where it is today. Had we been one or two months earlier it would have been great, because we were really very well situated — everybody said it was a no-brainer. But it was a very tough time because we had to lay off some people to keep things going.

It was then an obvious choice to sell the company. We may have made it, but it would have been very tough. We would have had to lay off more people and things like that. Selling to Pinnacle seemed like a good idea because they were from a different area — video — and this term is heavily used, but *synergy* was the effect we were really after. But it turned out to be really very chaotic, which is a pity because they had some really good companies, like the FAST people in Germany, and Miro. So we started to work on making a program that was actually a video and audio editor at the same time, something still really missing today. It could have been pretty good — the idea was good. But the company was very chaotic.

Given the success of Cubase, why was Nuendo developed?

CS: Nuendo was mainly a product for big studios, because synchronization is an important issue, and also 9-pin control — these things that are dedicated to big studios. So we saw that there was Pro Tools and Cubase was more targeted to composers and musicians. And Nuendo was a totally separate program initially. Only later did Nuendo and Cubase have a common code base. Cubase code was getting kind of old and messy, so later it migrated to that new code base.

Nuendo was meant for recording that is not so much bars-and-beats-oriented as time based. You could do it with Cubase, but then you had additional issues like time code control, synchronization, machine control. And Nuendo also did surround.

How do you deal with legacy code and keep the code modern?

CS: It's an ongoing process. If you have something that is, say, messy — you encapsulate it and make an object, you know? The initial code was assembler code; you couldn't do anything with it. But today you have C++ and object-oriented programming and all that, so it's a constantly evolving process. It still is today.

Because Cubase still had a lot of really old code, we were constantly trying to clean it up, and that was a lot of work. In a way, it's not so bad to sometimes say, "We'll do it from scratch." The work is not only the coding, but also developing the ideas and knowing what issues relate to them. You don't have to do all that again because you know what the issues are, so it's just a mater of putting it in a different form. And that still happens today, because code is always old—it's old by the time you write it.

Is there anything you wish you had done differently with Cubase?

MR: I think in general everything with Cubase was done right. A lot of stuff in Cubase these days is feedback from people using it over the years. It's not all just coming from Steinberg or Steinberg people. A lot of ideas were brought to Steinberg from people making music at all levels. Of course Hans Zimmer wanted zillions of features in there, but there are many people who want to have some specialized features in there, and that's why it's so feature rich these days. It wasn't really a goal in the beginning, but I think it came with the Internet and the Cubase community. These people really brought a lot to the table.

Are either of you still involved with the company in any way?

MR: No.

CS: I think I left when Yamaha took over. I'm still there occasionally doing some stuff, but it's a loose relationship.

How does it feel to be company founders on the outside looking in?

CS: I'm very happy that Yamaha took it over because they are from the business. As I've said, we were really aiming at a synergy with Pinnacle, and there were promises. It could have been a good thing, but just wasn't. So, it's much better that Yamaha is now steering the ship.

And what are you doing today?

MR: The thing we still do together, Charlie and I, is Digital Musician [www.digitalmusician.net], which is making music over the Internet.

CS: I wrote the software, which is a tool where you can record and do things on an FTP server or e-mail, where you send audio files. You can drag your files from your favorite DAW to our software, and everybody else gets it. You can also connect to somebody with picture and sound, and you can record. It's a lot of work.

MR: The idea is to get back to the roots of making music. If I want to have a great guitar player, I go on the Web and say, "Here is my song, would you like to play something on it?" So I can get a really great guitar part from somebody, wherever they are, instead of me fiddling around with a plug-in or something. It's really a scenario where someone playing live adds so much more to my composition than I can do with whatever tools I have. Even if I have a great string library in my computer, a real arranger will do a better job than I will. So it brings us back to collaboration.

Do you still play?

MR: Yes, absolutely, but not professionally. Charlie plays professionally.

CS: I'm in a band called Steer. The singer is an actor in some TV series in Germany, so quite a lot of people know his face. It's an interesting thing. I'm playing keyboards. I play guitar on one song, but they keep switching my amp off! [*Laughs*] Just kidding.

What do you think is the next big development in computer music?

MR: I think interacting with other people will become big, maybe not for my generation of musicians, but for the next generation. I think it's the same with Facebook and all these social communities—you don't really know these people. But you know a little about them, and you can do something. "Okay, he plays guitar." You don't know how old he is, maybe his picture looks very young or whatever. Maybe his brother plays guitar, and it's not even him. Doesn't matter. I think the next generation is more used to that, and it's fun to do this stuff over the Internet with all these people. I've got a great drummer in London. I don't know how old he is, but once he starts playing you know that he has played for many, many years. So I've replaced all my machine drums with his stuff. It's great.

CS: I agree. I think collaboration is a big issue. It takes very long, but everything is very much pointing in that direction: social networking and Web 2.0 stuff. I'm pretty certain there is a lot to come there.

One thing I always wished to have is a mixing thing where mixing is a bit different. For instance, you take a mix and say, "Okay, I can't really hear the singer very well because the frequency range is already covered by guitars and keyboards and things like that." Currently there is no tool that visualizes that or gets you to mix by shifting those frequencies. It's a rough idea. Call it "spectral mixing," if you will. I should write that down [laughs]. Anything spectral is interesting because it's an area that has not evolved yet.

Also, I've always wanted a mode in the mixer where you push a button and from that point on when you raise a fader everything else goes down. Like relative mixing; because you go to a studio and the guitarist says, "I can't hear the guitar," so the engineer pushes the guitar. Then the bass player says he can't hear the bass. So you end up with all the faders being up, and you should be able to [do it so that when you] raise the bass everything else goes down. I think in that area there are still some things to come.

50 Tips and Tricks for Cubase 5

By now you know that Cubase 5 is an incredibly deep program, developed over the course of 25 years to become a powerful platform for many types of music production. And while the new additions in Cubase 5 were covered in detail in chapters 1–6, there are hundreds of other features, functions, and procedures that can help you use Cubase more effectively and efficiently. This bonus chapter contains 50 tips, tricks, and suggestions to help you work faster, make Cubase run more efficiently, and help you get the most from Cubase 5.

I. Templates

Cubase gives you the ability to use templates, which are preset starting points for your project. These can store tracks, effects, instruments, and routing setups. Projects can be saved as templates by going to File > Save as Templates. Templates can be set up for different types of work such as mastering, live tracking, scoring, and mixing in surround, and will greatly speed up your workflow.

2. Project Folder

It's important to keep your recorded audio files organized. Cubase asks you to set up a Record folder when starting a new project.

A good rule of thumb is to have each song or project in its own folder. This simplifies file management, as similarly named audio files, such as bass, guitar, or vocals from other projects, do not get mixed up. This also makes it easier to archive projects, as all the files for one project are in a common folder.

3. Naming Tracks

It's common to have 40, 80, or even more than 100 audio files in a project; these can easily get disorganized and lost. Ideally, you'll want to name each track in the track list before recording. This track name will then be applied to the audio files in the track, and prevents having many audio files on your hard drive named "Audio 01."

4. Inserts vs. Effects Channels

There are two different ways of routing effects in Cubase: inserts and effects channels (also known as effects sends), which can lead to confusion. Inserts should be used for routing effects to a particular channel, and effects channels should be used for effects shared on several channels. Generally, EQs and compressors are used as inserts while reverbs and delays are used as effects channels. Reverbs are often the most demanding on CPU power, so instead of using reverb as an insert on multiple tracks, an effects channel lets multiple channels be sent to a single reverb instance. From there, the wet to dry ratio can be adjusted on each individual channel with the send level.

5. Mouse Right Click

Cubase offers context-sensitive functionality by simply right-clicking on your mouse. Mac users with a single-button mouse can enable the single to dual mouse button in the System Preferences. Right-clicking can allow customization of the transport bar, the upper toolbar, and the main tools in the Project window and MIDI and sample editors.

6. REVerence Expanded

The new reverb plug-in REVerence is a powerful convolution reverb that uses samples of actual environments to achieve incredibly realistic-sounding reverb. There are over 70 different environments included with REVerence, but it can be easily expanded. Multiple Web pages such as www.noisevault.com have many impulses available for download as standard WAV or AIFF files. Click on the Import button to load the WAV or AIFF files, and you can have many additional sounds for REVerence. REVerence is discussed in detail in chapter 4.

7. Multiple Time Displays

The time values in Cubase are all based on sample position, but can be displayed in multiple formats such as time, bars and beats, samples, or SMPTE time code position. The primary time display is set in the transport bar on the left-hand side. You can change the time display format by clicking in the primary time display section. Ruler tracks can be added anywhere in the Project window to show different time formats, so that audio tracks can be viewed under time and MIDI tracks under bars and beats.

8. SMPTE Generation

The Society of Motion Picture and Television Engineers (SMPTE) developed a time code to be used as a reference to synchronize multiple devices together. Cubase can synchronize to SMPTE time code from external devices, but this often requires an expensive hardware synchronizer. Alternatively, Cubase can act as the master device by generating its own SMPTE time code via a SMPTE generator plug-in found in the Tools plug-in folder. Add a mono audio track and select the SMPTE insert plug-in, then create a dedicated mono output bus in VST Connections. When Cubase plays, SMPTE time code will then be generated so that other devices can be synchronized with Cubase serving as the sync master.

9. Finding Files in MediaBay

A project can contain thousands of individual files, making it hard to organize and find them on your system. MediaBay is a database file-management system for organizing your audio files, MIDI loops, MIDI files, track presets, video files, and project files. The Browser on the left-hand side is a file directory indicating what folders or network locations are available. The Viewer pane in the center shows categories and search results, and the Tag Editor allows metadata to be added into a file. For example, you can find a rock guitar track preset by selecting the Track Preset icon at the top of the Viewer pane, selecting the category Guitar/Plucked and subcategory of E, then selecting Guitar and Rock/Metal under Style. MediaBay will then show you all of the files on your system, regardless of where they are stored, that match this criteria. Searches for other types of files are handled in the same way, making it a fast and easy way to search your system for content. MediaBay is discussed in detail in chapter 5.

10. Project Setup

Cubase can record different audio file formats, sample rates, and bit depths. These settings can be adjusted under Project > Project Setup. This is a centralized location to set defaults for the time display, SMPTE frame rate, audio file bit depth and sample rate, pan law, and record file format.

11. Audio Interface Setup

Cubase can work with virtually any audio interface, using ASIO for low-latency communication and Core Audio on the Mac OS. Cubase generally defaults to a PC or Mac's onboard audio interface until you select the driver for the audio interface. Go to Device Menu > Device Setup and select VST Audio System. In the ASIO driver, select the audio interface to route audio from Cubase to your audio interface.

12. Setting Up Inputs and Outputs

The inputs and outputs for your audio interface can be configured in the VST Connections window under Devices > VST Connections. Here you will find tabs for inputs, outputs, studio, etc. Cubase generally defaults to a stereo I/O for your audio interface. If you need more inputs or outputs, simply select the appropriate tab and click the Add Bus button. The channel configuration allows mono, stereo, or surround tracks, and number selects the number of channels to be added. Select the physical output of the interface in the Device Ports column. The physical connection(s) to an audio interface can be used multiple times. For example, an 8-channel interface can be configured as 8 mono, 4 stereo, or 5.1 surround plus stereo tracks. The newly created inputs will then be visible for routing. Input and output configurations can be stored as user presets by clicking on the "+" sign to the right of the presets selection.

13. Fades and Crossfades

Among the most common audio edits are fades and crossfades. You can perform these edits quickly and easily right in the Cubase Project window. Selecting an audio part will show you five anchor points: one in each corner and one in the upper center. The top left and right handles are the fade-in and fade-out handles. Moving these handles in over the audio part creates linear fades. The fades can be edited by double-clicking in the fade area. The fade points can be manually added by adding points or by using one of the fade presets built into Cubase. Crossfades are used to make seamless transitions between edits. To do this, overlap two different audio parts and hit the X key. This fades out the first part and fades in the second part. The crossfade can be resized by adjusting the boundaries and edited by double-clicking on it.

14. Offline Processing

Cubase can run many real-time effects, but it can also apply effects and sample editing offline. The advantage of this is that the file will then be processed and will not take up additional DSP resources. Sample Editor processes such as Normalize, Gain, Fades, and Remove DC Offset are applied by going to Audio > Process. Plug-ins can be applied in the same manner by going to Audio > Plug-ins.

15. Offline Process History

Cubase offers unlimited levels of undo in the project until it is saved or closed. The Offline Process History allows the offline processes to be undone in a nonlinear fashion even after saving the project. Select the audio and go to Audio > Offline Process History, and all offline processes are shown. Select any process and it can be individually removed or changed without affecting the other processes in the list.

16. Zooming Options

Cubase has many zooming methods to make navigating your project or the editors easier. You can use the H and G keys to zoom in horizontally. Vertical and horizontal zoom controls are located in the bottom right-hand corner, as well as presets. One of the best ways of zooming is to use the drop zoom method. Move the cursor to the primary time display, hold the left mouse button down, and move the cursor straight up and down. The tracks will quickly zoom in and out.

17. Instrument Rack vs. Instrument Tracks

There are two different ways of adding VST instruments to a Cubase project: as an instrument track or as part of the instrument rack. Instruments can be loaded into the VST instruments rack by going to Devices > VST Instruments. Instruments loaded into the VST instrument rack can be assigned to an existing MIDI track, and that MIDI track can then be reassigned to any other MIDI device. Instruments loaded into the VST instrument rack can also be multitimbral, meaning they can play back multiple sounds on different MIDI channels, if that is supported by the instrument. The audio outputs are also separate and not directly tied to the MIDI track. Instrument tracks are not multitimbral, and the audio output is automatically routed to the instrument track, making it a bit cleaner and better organized. Instrument tracks cannot be changed to another MIDI source. In general, instrument tracks are a bit easier to use and more organized, but offer less flexibility and lack the multitimbral options offered by instruments in the VST instrument rack.

18. Drag-and-Drop Inserts

You can quickly change the order of inserts on a track by dragging them to rearrange the order. This can change the sound dramatically, especially with dynamics plug-ins. There are icons to the right of the inserts labeled i1 – i8 for the 8 inserts. Select an icon and simply move it up or down to another insert to change the order.

19. Remote Controllers

Cubase supports many different controllers such as Mackie Control, or digital consoles like the Yamaha O2R96v2 so that you can use physical faders and knobs to control functions in the software. Cubase also offers a Generic Remote Control so that any device that transmits MIDI data can be set up as a controller. Controllers can be set up under Devices > Device Setup by clicking on the big "+" sign in the upper left-hand corner. Select the remote control and define the MIDI input and output ports where the controller is connected to the computer.

20. External Hardware Effects Integration

Cubase includes a wide variety of software effect plug-ins, but it can easily integrate external hardware processing with delay compensation. This makes incorporating an external hardware compressor or reverb as easy as adding a software plug-in. Connect the external processor to the inputs of your audio interface. Go to Devices > VST Connections and select the External FX tab.

Select Add External FX, name the effect, and select the channel configuration. Go to an insert or effects channel track and select the effect from the External Plug-in list. A dialog box appears with an icon in the upper center section. Clicking the icon will automatically measure the latency of the signal path so that the signal to the processor is perfectly in time.

21. Direct Monitoring: On or Off?

Audio interfaces impose *latency*, the delay that an audio signal takes to go from the input to the output when working with Cubase. Latency can be set in the control panel for the audio interface and is expressed as a buffer size or in milliseconds. Lowering the buffer adds more strain on the computer. The latency is noticeable if you are monitoring audio as it is being recorded. If effects like reverb and compression are added to the audio track, the latency is compounded and can throw off a musician's timing with a delayed sound. Many audio interfaces offer direct monitoring or the ability to pass the signal directly from the input to the output, bypassing the software audio engine. This can make it easier for the person being recorded, but it will bypass the software audio engine and effects. Direct monitoring can be turned on or off by going to Devices > Device Setup and selecting the audio interface under the VST Audio System.

22. Multi-Output VST Instruments

Many software instruments like Steinberg's HALion sampler offer multiple outputs to the mixer so that different sounds can be distributed across multiple faders and mixed separately. Cubase defaults to loading a single stereo output to the mixer. To set up an instrument's multi-output capabilities, first load an instrument into the VST instrument rack in Devices > VST Instruments. There is an icon just to the left of the instrument name in the VST instrument rack. Click on the icon, and a pop-up dialog box appears with all the available outputs for the instrument. Once the outputs have been activated they will immediately show up in the mixer.

23. VST Plug-in Folder in Cubase Windows

VST plug-ins on the Windows platform can be installed into any folder on the computer. It is a good idea to have a common folder for VST plug-ins, but some plug-ins are automatically installed into separate folders. If your plug-ins are not visible in Cubase, go to Devices > Plug-in Information and click on the VST 2.x Plug-in Paths button. Select the Add button and select the folder in the browser window. Hit the Update button, and the plug-ins are now accessible in Cubase.

24. Undo History

Cubase offers unlimited levels of undo and redo until the project is closed or saved. The standard key commands Control/Command + Z will undo all edits, and Control/Command + Shift + Z will redo all edits sequentially. The Edit History is displayed by going to Edit > History. You can cycle through the edit history by moving the mouse up and down the list.

25. Key Commands

Cubase has hundreds of keyboard shortcuts for various functions in the program. You can greatly speed up your workflow by learning the available key commands. Many menu functions have the key command indicated next to the function. Key commands can be controlled by going to File > Key Commands. Key commands can also be searched by typing the text in the black dialog box at the top and hitting the magnifying glass icon. Key commands can also be easily customized. To do this, select the function, click the black text box under it, enter the key command, and click Assign.

26. Macros

Macros speed up workflow for repetitive functions and procedures. A macro is a series of key commands that run sequentially to complete a task. For example, a repetitive task that contains seven steps can be done as a single macro. Macros are created by going to File > Key Commands and selecting Show Macros. Select the New Macro button, select the first key command function, and choose Add Command. Double-click on the untitled macro to name it. The macros can be run by selecting Edit > Macros.

27. Optimizing VST3 Plug-in Performance

VST3 is the latest generation of Steinberg's acclaimed cross-platform technology, and offers many benefits such as surround capability, remote support, and settings to optimize system performance. Many times a project requires different plug-ins to be used for different sections of a song. For example, if the chorus of your song contains background vocals that are not found in the verse, you'll want to bypass any plug-ins used on that track during the verse to save CPU power. Cubase has a preference that will automatically bypass any plug-ins when they receive no audio. Go to Preferences > VST Plug-ins and check the box marked "Suspend VST3 plug-in processing when no audio signals are received." This can greatly expand the processing power of plug-ins used in a project.

28. Track Presets

Storing track presets is an easy way to speed up your workflow. A track preset contains the volume, pan, EQ, inserts, and phase settings for a track, and can be stored and recalled in any project. A track preset is ideal when seeking consistency throughout a project. For example, if the same bass layer is used on multiple sessions, a track preset containing these settings can be easily stored and recalled, making it quick and easy to get this sound back. To create a track preset, right-click on the track, select Create Track Preset, and type in a name. If the Tag Editor button is activated, additional metadata can be stored for the preset. To recall a track preset, simply add a track and select Browse Presets.

29. Project Archival and Migration

Archiving and migrating projects from Cubase was once a time-consuming process that often involved soloing each track and exporting them one at a time. Most applications run different effects and virtual instruments, so it is sometimes impossible to open a project in another program. The new Batch Export function in Cubase simplifies this process, allowing all elements of a project to be exported simultaneously as equal-length audio files. Set the left and right locators around the whole project by selecting all of the parts and hitting the P key. Go to File > Export > Audio Mixdown and select Batch Export. Check all of the individual elements that should be included, such as Outputs, Groups, FX Channels, Instrument Tracks, VST Instruments, and Audio Channels. Select the path where the new files should be saved to and hit Export. The files will be copied to a new folder and will all be the same length. Import all the files into any other application, and all the files will start at the same time.

30. Change the Speed

Cubase offers incredibly powerful real-time audio stretching so that an audio file can be played back slower or faster. There are two modes to play back audio—musical and linear. Musical mode shifts the playback position of audio and MIDI based on the tempo, whereas linear mode uses the actual time positions as the playback position basis. Cubase defaults to musical mode but that can be changed by clicking on the quarter-note icon in the track settings so that it looks like a clock. Audio Warp allows the tempo to be changed freely after recording, but Cubase needs to have an original tempo to start. Cubase automatically applies the current project tempo as the original tempo to audio files as they are recorded. Go to the Audio Pool Media > Open Pool Window and select the View/Attributes icon. Make sure that Tempo and Musical Mode are both checked, and check the Musical Mode icon for all audio files. Play the project and change the tempo in the transport bar and listen to the music change accordingly.

31. Find the Tempo

With its sophisticated tempo mapping, Cubase is a powerful tool for working on film compositions or remixes. Time Warp creates a tempo map from an existing musical performance, whether it's recorded in MIDI or audio. This allows for MIDI parts or drum loops to follow the tempo of existing tracks. Activate the Tempo icon on the transport bar and select the Time Warp tool from the main toolbar. Set the main time display to bars and beats mode. Move a rhythmically significant part, such as a kick drum, to the top track directly below the timeline. Move the Time Warp tool directly below the main timeline, and while holding down the Shift key, move the barline to the downbeat of the audio file. Continue this for each measure throughout the song, and a tempo map will be created.

32. Tune Vocals

One of the new features in Cubase 5 is VariAudio, which allows you to correct the pitch of monophonic audio files and edit them similarly to the way MIDI information is edited in the key editor. Double-click on the audio file to open the sample editor and select the VariAudio tab in the Inspector on the left-hand side. Select the icon to the left of the Pitch & Warp selection to start the analysis. Once the analysis is complete, the audio file will now be displayed graphically. Click on a note to hear it individually and move it with the mouse to have it snap to the correct pitch. Using the up/down arrow keys on your computer keyboard can change the pitch by semitones; use the left/right arrow keys to navigate to the previous or next note. Entire phrases can be "pitch quantized" or moved to the nearest pitch by adjusting the Pitch Quantize slider to the right. The vibrato of a note can be minimized or erased by using the Straighten Pitch slider. VariAudio is discussed in detail in chapter 3.

33. Drag-and-Drop Drums

Groove Agent One is an MPC-style drum machine included with Cubase 5 that has some unique integration features. Audio files from the Project window or MediaBay can be dragged and dropped directly onto one of the pads and then triggered as MIDI events. Groove Agent One can also go a step further with its loop deconstruction features as well. Go to a drum loop and double-click on it to launch the sample editor, then select the Hitpoints tab. Move the slider sensitivity until each rhythmically significant beat has a hitpoint associated with it. Click on the slice and close icon. Drag the sliced audio file to one of the Groove Agent One pads while holding down the Shift key. Each slice is now placed on a separate pad. In the Exchange section of Groove Agent One, select the two arrows and drag it to a MIDI track in Cubase. A MIDI part is now created that plays back the individual MIDI notes of the original loop. The loop can be deconstructed in the MIDI editor to get fast, simple variations without artifacts. Groove Agent One is discussed in detail in chapter 2.

34. Beat Making

Creating beats can be great way to get inspiration for a song. A new MIDI plug-in in Cubase 5 called Beat Designer makes creating beats fast and easy. Go to a MIDI track and route the output to a MIDI drum sound. Then, go to the Inspector, select MIDI inserts, and open Beat Designer. A step sequencer view becomes visible. Click in the grid to add notes. Velocity can be adjusted by moving the mouse up and down on the note. Clicking in the very bottom of the note adds flams, which can be adjusted in the lower left-hand corner. There are two independent swing factors with adjustments on the right-hand sliders, allowing notes to be shifted ahead of or behind the beat. The programmed beat can be brought into the main Cubase Project window by selecting the options found under the arrow icon in the upper left-hand corner. Beat Designer is discussed in detail in chapter 2.

35. Alternate Tool Functions

The Cubase Toolbox offers simple-to-use tools such as Scissors, Eraser, Glue, etc. Most of these tools offer extended functionality when using the modifier keys Alt on Windows and Option on

Mac. Pressing the Alt/Option key, using the Selection tool and going to the lower right-hand corner and dragging the part to the right makes quick copies. Holding down the Alt/Option key and using the Scissors will make similar-sized cuts until the end of the part. The Alt/Option key used with the Glue tool will join cut parts together to the end of the part. The Eraser tool erases all the following parts on a track when clicking on a part with the Alt/Option key pressed.

36. Motif XS Integration

The merging of Yamaha and Steinberg over four years ago has brought significantly improved functionality and hardware integration, including for the popular Motif XS keyboard workstation. The Motif XS offers great sounds, effects, and arpeggios, and several downloads for it are available on www. yamahasynth.com, such as a USB driver, extensions, and VST editor. The USB driver allows the Motif to communicate with Cubase over a USB connection without the need for a traditional MIDI interface. The extensions allow the Motif XS to act as a controller and for a motif .all song file to be imported directly into Cubase. The biggest benefit of the hardware integration is that you can select patches and edit sounds and effects within the Motif XS from the VST software editor, and all of the settings will be instantly recalled with the Cubase project. The Motif XS can be treated like a virtual instrument while handling all its own processing internally, avoiding strain on the computer.

37. Display Quantize

Viewing musical notation from a recorded MIDI part on a sequencer is problematic unless the part has been quantized. Notation programs like to see the notes directly on the beat for accuracy. However, quantizing can often throw off the natural feel of the part. Many people who rely on printed notation have to create one track for playback with natural timing and a separate track for notation that is rigidly quantized. The score editor in Cubase features Display Quantize to resolve this dilemma. In the score editor, go to Scores > Open Selection. Go to Scores > Settings and open the Score Settings dialog. Select the Staff tab and then the Main subtab. In Display Quantize set the notes and rest values to the smallest rhythmic note of the part. The appearance of the notation will be quantized for accuracy while the actual sequenced notes are left in the same position for natural-sounding playback.

38. Chord Charts

Many musicians use lead sheets in the studio or live as a musical guideline to indicate the chord changes in their song. Cubase can quickly generate lead sheets for a part. Select a part that contains chords, such as a piano part. In the score editor, go to Scores > Open Selection. Select all of the notes (Edit > Select > All) and then go to Scores > Make Chord Symbols.

39. Page Mode vs. Edit Mode

The notation display in Cubase can be viewed in two different modes: page mode and edit mode. Edit mode is designed for altering notes and rhythms of notes. Page mode shows how the page is displayed for printing. Page mode also offers a Layout tool, which lets you move the notation graphically without affecting the rhythmic value of the notes. Right-click to select the Layout tool.

40. Score Settings

The most commonly needed settings for handling notation can be found in the Score Settings dialog. Go to Scores > Settings or double-click just to the left of the stave in the score editor. The Project tab is where you set the font, accidentals, and chord display symbols. The Layout tab is where you lay out the part to be adjusted with size and consolidated rests. The Staff tab handles display quantize, guitar tablature, key and clef, as well as orchestral transposition. The Text tab is where you set the fonts and the sizes for text used in the score.

4I. Folder Tracks

Cubase projects often contain many tracks, and organizing them visually is difficult. Folder tracks help you to organize your tracks in a logical way. For example, if your project contains multiple drums, guitars, keyboard parts, and vocals, each of these can be grouped together in a folder. You add a folder track by right-clicking on the track list and selecting Add Folder Track. Double-click on the folder and name it. Select the first track to be placed in the folder, hold down the Shift key, and select the last track. Now, grab the tracks and move them to the folder track until a green arrow pointing left appears, then let go. The folder can be collapsed or expanded by clicking on the folder icon or by going to Project > Track Folding > Toggle Selected Tracks. Folder tracks can be edited like other parts in the Project window, and can also be nested to have multiple folders within a master folder track.

42. Volume Control

There are three quick ways to adjust the volume of an audio part from the Project window in Cubase. The easiest way to adjust the volume is with the clip-based volume handle. Select the audio clip and move the handle (the blue square) in the center up or down to adjust the volume. The second way is by selecting the Draw tool and drawing volume changes into the clip. The third way is by drawing in volume automation. To do this, first open the automation lane. Move the cursor to the bottom left-hand corner of the track name column until an arrow is visible, and click on it. Use the Draw or Line tool to enter the volume automation data.

43. MIDI Timing Offset in Windows

There are several MIDI timing engines for Windows, which may cause your MIDI tracks to be stacked or offset earlier after recording. This issue can be remedied by going into Device > Device Setup > MIDI > MIDI Port Setup. Check the option "Use system timestamp for Windows MIDI inputs."

44. Speaker Switching and Monitoring

It is typical to use several sets of speakers when mixing. Many people purchase hardware devices or use a console to switch between speakers, but Cubase's Control Room feature handles this easily. You can set up the control room by going to Devices > VST Connections > Studio. Right-click and select Add Monitor. Choose the output connection of the audio interface where the speakers are connected. It is important to go to the Outputs tab and set the same outputs, so the audio is not sent to two different destinations. Set up all your monitors in this way, whether in 5.1 surround or mono. To switch between speakers, go to Devices > VST Control Room Mixer and click the A/B icon in the lower right-hand corner. Also note that the fader in the control room mixer serves as a master volume control and does not affect the gain structure set by the master fader in Cubase.

45. Headphone Mixes

Headphone mixes provide the musicians in a session with a dedicated mix in their headphones while recording. However, a singer may need to hear a different headphone or cue mix than the drummer. The Control Room in Cubase makes it easy to set up headphone mixes. You can add headphone mixes for the Control Room by going to Devices > VST Connections > Studio, then right-click and select Add Studio. The Studios can be named. Connect the headphones to the headphone output of your audio interface or connect the outputs of your audio interface to a headphone amplifier. Select an audio track in the track Inspector and open the Studio Sends tab. If it is not visible, right-click on one of the tabs in the Inspector and select Studio Sends so that a check mark is visible. Turn on the button for the studio send and move the slider toward the right. This sends varying amounts of the selected track to each of the headphone mixes.

46. Side Chaining

Side chaining allows an audio track to serve as the input source for dynamics processing. A common example of this is to have a music bed "duck" under a voiceover or have a kick drum control the dynamics of a bass track. Side chaining can be set up in Cubase by placing a dynamics plug-in, such as the Compressor, on the track you want to be compressed. Open the plug-in and click on the Activate Side Chain icon found just to the left of the black-label area of the plug-in. Go to the track that you want to key or control the output of the plug-in, and in the outputs, select the side chain. The outputs for the side chain can also be set from the sends.

47. Scoring to Video

Cubase is widely used for scoring film and TV shows. A video can be imported into a project on a video track and be integrated into the same timeline as the audio and MIDI. A thumbnail track is automatically created. Going to Devices > Video Window opens a video window for viewing while working. The Windows platform offers several different types of video playback engines. If there is no video present in Windows, try switching the video playback engine by going to Devices > Device Setup and selecting Video Player. Scoring to video is very simple using the Time Warp tool. Move the start measure to the desired point in the video. Select the number of bars and stretch the measures while holding down the Shift key using the Time Warp tool. The time of the tempo now changes so that the measures line up evenly with the video cue.

48. Vocal Character

The new Pitch Correct plug-in in Cubase offers some interesting functions besides correcting the intonation of vocals. In the formant section, select the gender of the singer and leave formant preservation on. Raising the values in the Shift dialog can make the singer sound younger, while lowering the values can make them sound older. This is great for making interesting changes to the character of a vocal. Pitch Correct is discussed in detail in chapter 3.

49. Quick Controls

The Quick Controls tab in the track Inspector allows you to set up "shortcuts" for up to eight different parameters in a track. It can act as a control center for things like remote controllers or be used to control automation, but in its most simple form it can set up a "mini-mixer" for each track. To do this, open the Quick Controls tab and click in the first empty slot. Double-click on the parameter you want to control and repeat for up to eight slots. You now have shortcuts for up to eight parameters that can be quickly accessed in the Inspector.

50. Preparing for Audio CD or MP3

While Cubase records and mixes music on your computer, most people listening to your music will not have the luxury of hearing it in your studio, so you'll need to prepare the files for distribution as an MP3 file or audio CD. Cubase can internally mix down all the audio, MIDI instruments, effects, and automation in your project to a stereo audio file. To do this, select all of the parts in the project (Edit > Select All) and hit the letter P on your keyboard, which sets the left and right locators around the entire song. Go to File > Export Audio Mixdown, and select the Main Stereo Output or Master Out. Give the file a name and choose where it should be saved in the Path location. In the file format, choose WAV or AIFF, set the sample rate to 44.100 kHz, choose 16-bit in the bit depth field, and hit Export. You can create MP3s the same way, except you select MPEG-1 Layer 3 in the file format and choose the compression ratio with the bit-rate slider.

Index